THIRD EDITION

JAZZ ENGLISH
Real Conversations
Real Improvement

1

**NO RULES
JUST SPEAKING
LONG & LOUD**

GUNTHER BREAUX

Compass Publishing

JAZZ ENGLISH 1 Third Edition

Gunther Breaux

© 2015 Compass Publishing

All rights reserved. No part of this book may be reproduced, stored in a retrieval system, or transmitted in any form by any means, electronic, mechanical, photocopying, recording, or otherwise without prior permission from the publisher.

Acquisitions Editor: Peggy Anderson
Editor: Daniel Deacon
Design and layout: Gunther Breaux

ISBN: 978-89-6697-858-8

20 19 18 17 16 15
26 25

Photo Credits: pp. 18, 21, 29, 30, 34, 37, 45, 50 © courtesy of Gunther Breaux
pp. 21, 22, 26, 29, 38, 42, 46, 53, 58, 61, 62, 69, 78 © Shutterstock
pp. 38, 66, 70 © iStock
pp. 29, 74 © Corel Corporation
p. 77 © Courtesy of Hye-in Jung

Websites: compasspub.com, jazzenglish.com

Every effort has been made to trace all sources of illustrations/photos/information in this book, but if any have been inadvertently overlooked, the publisher will be pleased to make the necessary arrangements at the first opportunity.

Printed in Korea

THIS BOOK IS ABOUT YOU.

There are over 300 questions in this book.

You know the answers because every question is about you.

Just write your answers and use them to speak.

Think of this book as the dialog to the English movie of your life.

ACKNOWLEDGMENTS

Chris Kobylinski has greatly enhanced this book. His knowledge of American and Korean culture, along with his teaching experience and expertise, make this book more interesting, authentic, and relevant. Daniel Deacon's contribution as editor includes much more than editing. His visual and artistic sense and teaching experience have helped every facet of this book. Also, Dan's British background broadens the relevance of this book.

Gratitude goes to my colleagues Jim Life, Mike Madill, Shaun Manning, and Todd Hull, who freely shared their expertise. I also appreciate the help given by the superb teachers and professors who use *Jazz English*: Jared Betts, Bryan Betz, Richard Cassidy, Katelyn Jones, Amelie Kelly, Robbie Sawlor, Ehren Schaiberger, Laurie Schulte, Nikki Slack, Marika Svaboda, and Jasmine Taiwo.

Finally, Kang Gui-lim's expertise in teaching methodology and layout design, her cultural insights, and her translating skills have immeasurably helped this book.

Gunther Breaux has taught English conversation in Korea for eighteen years. He's an associate professor at Hankuk University of Foreign Studies in Seoul and the author of several ELT books. He has a BA in Advertising Design, an MA in American History, and an MA in TESOL. For eleven years, he taught at Dongduk Women's University, and for five years he taught Business English part-time at the Korea Development Institute (KDI). He has also taught Computer Graphics at the Korea National University of the Arts.

CONTENTS

PREVIEW & INSTRUCTIONS   5

CHANGE THE MINDSET
First Week
    Real-World English   10
    Speed Dating   12

Second Week
    Classroom MT   14
    Personality Test   16

MAIN UNITS
  1 Family   18
  2 Hobbies & Interests   26
  3 University   34
  4 Shopping   42
  5 Movies   50
  6 Food & Restaurants   58
  7 Sports & Exercise   66
  8 Vacations & Travel   74

SUPPORT UNITS
  9 Pronunciation Practice & Konglish   82
  10 Describing   84
  11 Core Vocabulary   92
  12 Core Skills   96
  13 Explanations & Examples   99
  14 Board Games   124
  15 Maps: World, USA, Korea, Seoul   133

There are over 300 questions in this book. Each question is designed to start a conversation. You know the answers because every question is about you. Just write your answer and use it to speak.

PREVIEW

DO THE BOOK AT HOME, SPEAK IN CLASS.

Translated vocabulary   Pair activity: 16 conversation-starting questions   Model Conversation

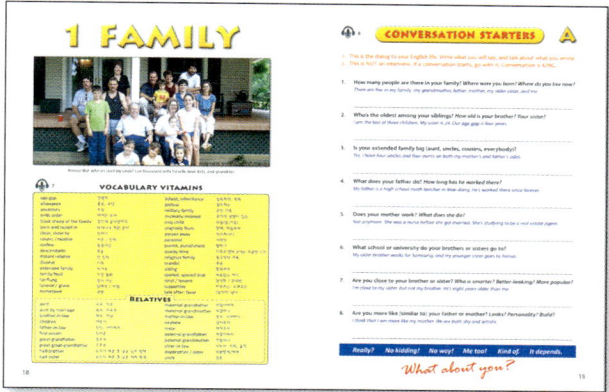
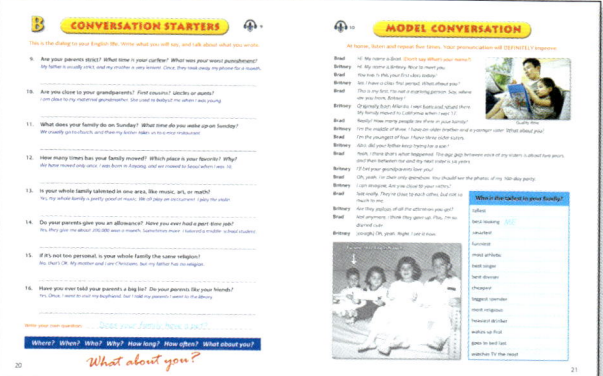

Top Cultural Differences and vocabulary crossword puzzle   Example paragraph for longer and better speaking   SPEAKING, SPEAKING, SPEAKING
Don't forget to breathe.

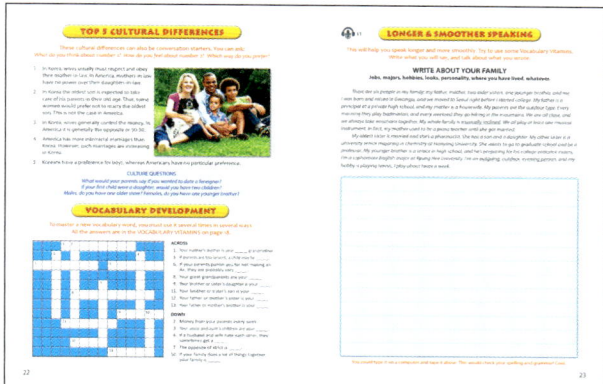
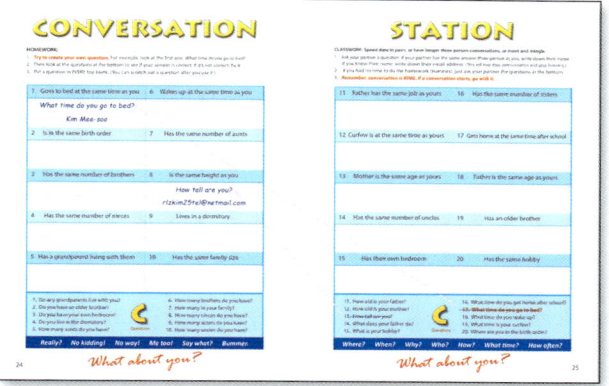

INSTRUCTIONS FOR STUDENTS

DO THE BOOK AT HOME, SPEAK IN CLASS.

Page 1:   Listen and pronounce the Vocabulary Vitamins. As you do, highlight some of the words that you like and will use later.

Pages 2 - 3:   Listen and pronounce. Then write your own answers, and try to use the new vocabulary. This is the English dialog to your life. Write what you will say, and talk about what you wrote.

Page 4:   Listen and pronounce—several times. Record yourself and listen.

Page 5:   Read the Cultural Differences. Do the crossword puzzle. All the answers to the puzzle are in the Vocabulary Vitamins. This will help integrate the new vocabulary. And it's fun.

Page 6:   Listen and pronounce the practice paragraph, and then write your own. This makes your speaking longer and smoother. Write what you will say, and talk about what you wrote.

Pages 7 - 8:   Construct sixteen conversation questions. This improves your thinking and speaking. (Conversations require questions.) Then you use the questions in your conversations.

 The icon for the audio files is earphones AND a microphone. Why?
To improve you must listen, repeat, record yourself, and listen to yourself.

5

INSTRUCTIONS FOR TEACHERS

PAGE 1: VOCABULARY VITAMINS

1. Strongly encourage students to bring in family photos. Korean wedding photos contain many family members.

2. Pronounce the vocabulary. Explain where needed or interesting. Make sure students know about the Explanations & Examples section at the back of the book.

3. The unit pretest is multiple-choice listening and covers vocabulary. Therefore, to do well on it, students must listen and know how the new vocabulary is pronounced.

PAGES 2 & 3: CONVERSATION STARTERS

1. Remind students that each question is meant to start a conversation.

2. Remind students to make comments (*Really? Me too! No way!*) and to ask follow-up questions (*Where, When, Why, Who? What about you?*).

3. The questions can be asked in any order the student chooses. However, students should understand and be able to answer all the questions.

4. Both students open the book. One asks page A questions, the other page B. Neither student can read the question they are being asked. This improves their listening.

5. In the third class period, to add variety, students can sit in groups of three. One student uses page A, one uses page B, and one uses the C pages, which are the last two pages of the unit.

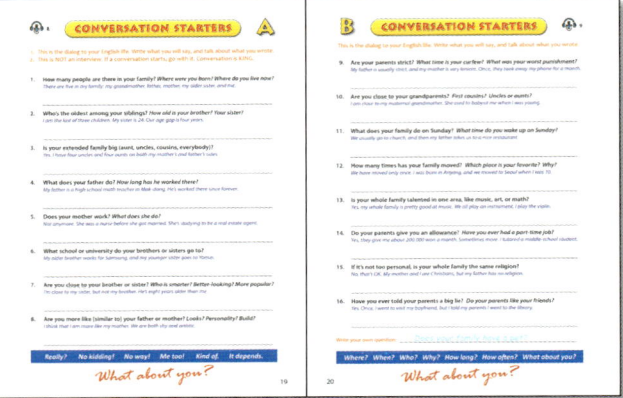

SPEED DATING: One interesting topic (me), many partners

1. Students sit in pairs, in straight rows. (If the rows are not straight, switching partners is chaotic.)

2. Every five to ten minutes, yell SWITCH! Remind students to say goodbye and hello: *Later, See you later, Gotta go, Nice to meet you. Hi, my name is Kim Min-soo. I like your hairdo.*

3. In one class, students will switch four to six times. In a class of twenty, they can switch nine times and never have the same partner again. That is three or four weeks without talking to the same person twice. VARIETY! If you explain your hobby nine times, you will surely improve.

4. If students tire of questions, or answers, they simply ask other questions.

5. By repeating common questions and answers, students get a variety of answers and a variety of ways that answers are pronounced.

6. If students' questions or answers are not understood, they can try different pronunciations until they find the one that works.

PAGE 4: MODEL CONVERSATION

1. This page gives students a natural conversation model.
2. Students are urged to listen and pronounce the audio, repeatedly.
3. Teachers can put the students in pairs to practice the dialogues.
4. There is often some kind of checklist to fill out. This is part of the homework check, and it also provides conversation starters.

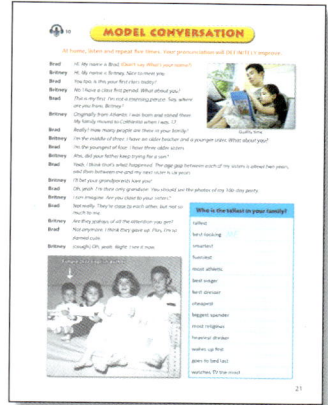

PAGE 5: TOP CULTURAL DIFFERENCES

1. Teachers can explain these. Perhaps they know of current movies that illustrate some of the differences.
2. The Cultural Differences can also be conversation starters.
3. The crossword puzzles are actually easy fill-in-the-blank vocabulary exercises (because you know exactly how many letters are in the answer). All the answers are in the Vocabulary Vitamins on the first page of each unit.

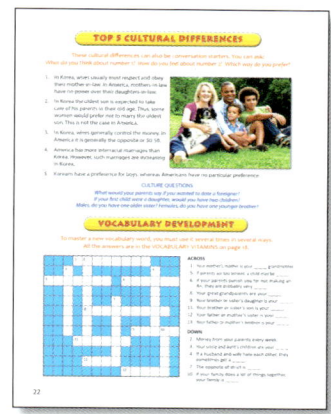

PAGE 6: SPEAKING AMMUNITION

1. Writing helps students speak longer and more smoothly.
2. The model helps them to write well-organized paragraphs.
3. Students should try to use Vocabulary Vitamins in their paragraphs.
4. They are encouraged to listen to the paragraph with the book closed first. Then they open the book and follow along. This improves listening.

PAGES 7 & 8: CONVERSATION STATION

1. The A and B pages at the beginning of the unit are for pair conversations. Conversation Station can be used as the C page in trio conversations.
2. For homework: At the top of each box is information that students want to get. To get that information, they must form and ask certain questions. For example, if the information is *Find someone's hobby*, students try to create the appropriate question: *"Are you have hobby?"* Then they check below and find that their question is incorrect. They should have used, *"Do you have a hobby?"*
3. In class, students can sit in groups of three. One student uses page A, one uses page B, and one uses these C pages.

DO THE BOOK AT HOME, SPEAK IN CLASS.

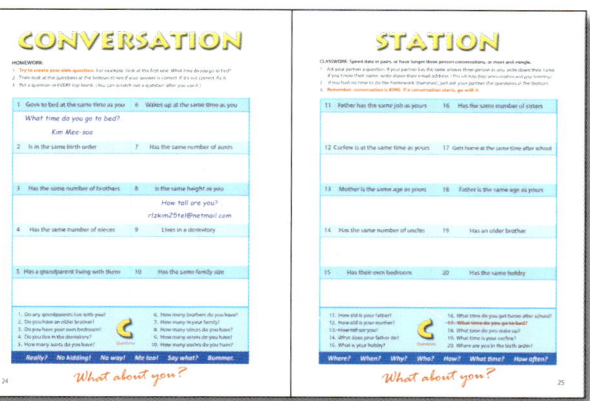

SUPPORT UNITS

1. **CORE VOCABULARY**: The vocabulary is translated and can be used to support any unit. When the electricity fails, you can pronounce one of these sheets.

    JOBS, PERSONALITY, and LOOKS are useful in **Unit 1: Family** for talking about family members.

    CLOTHING and LOOKS are good for **Unit 6: Shopping,** and Looks is also good for **Unit 5: Movies**.

2. **DESCRIBING, FREQUENCY, QUALITY, COMPARISON**:

    The DESCRIBING activity is for both males and females. What a hoot!

    In conversation, you also talk about how often you do something (FREQUENCY), how fun or awful it is (QUALITY), and how it is different from something else (COMPARISON).

3. **BOARD GAMES**: The board games in back can be used as often as you like. The Free Talking Frenzy game is a great ice-breaker on the first day of class. Later in the semester when interest is flagging, use the board games to spice things up. You could do the Free Talking game systematically: Do the blue questions one week, then the red, then the purple, then the green. Each color has a variety of questions.

4. **MAPS**: There are maps of Seoul, Korea, the USA, and the world. Maps are a great help when you are asked: *Where do you live? How do you get to school? What did you do last summer?*

72 questions in 4 colors
Do a different color every week.

200 Jazz Questions!
I kid you not.

KOREA
Where did you go last summer?

SEOUL
Where do you live?

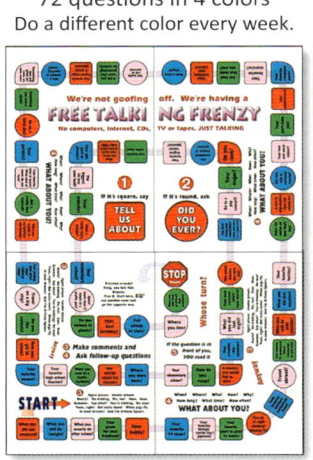 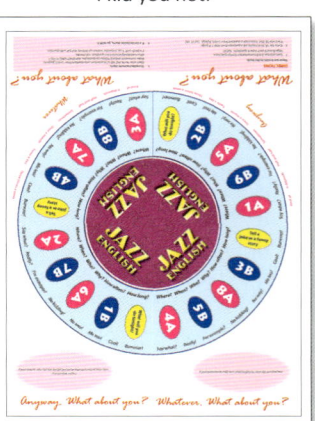 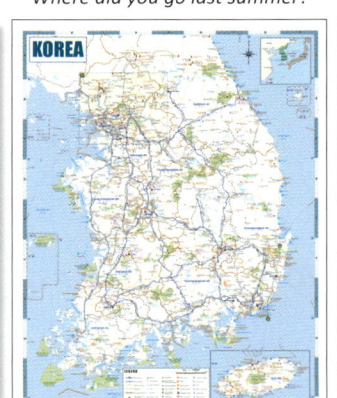 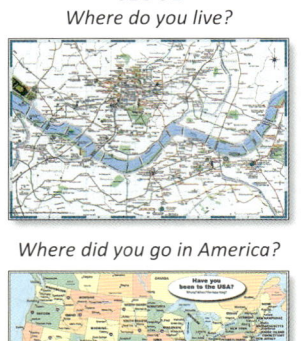

Where did you go in America?

THE CLASS: SPEED DATING

The engine of improvement is SPEED DATING. It provides FOCUS, VARIETY, and REPETITION.

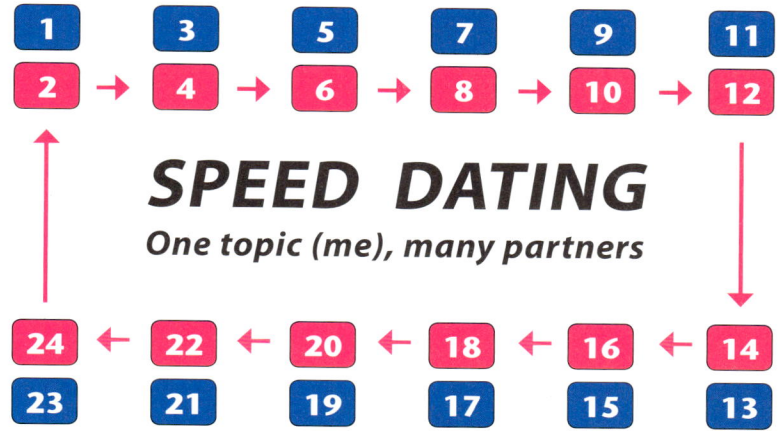

SPEED DATING
One topic (me), many partners

THE BIGGER THE CLASS, THE BETTER.
More partners = more variety = more interesting = more repetition = more improvement

IN BRIEF

1. **Pretest**: Students do the book at home and speak in class. The unit pretests force students to cover the book at home.
2. **First class**: SPEED DATE using the A and B pages. Students master hearing and answering the **BASICS**.
3. **Second class**: Speed date in pairs again, with new partners, getting **SMOOTHER** and **BETTER**.
Or use the A, B, and C pages—with new partners—for longer trio conversations. **VARIETY**.

1st CLASS

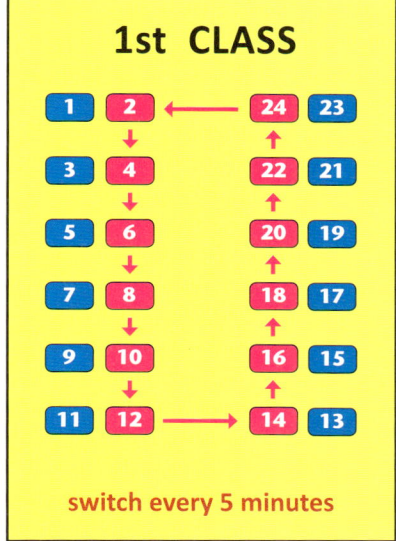

switch every 5 minutes

1. Students sit like so, odds with evens.
2. You yell **SPEAK**.
3. After five minutes, you yell **SWITCH**.
4. Odds stay, evens move.

2nd CLASS

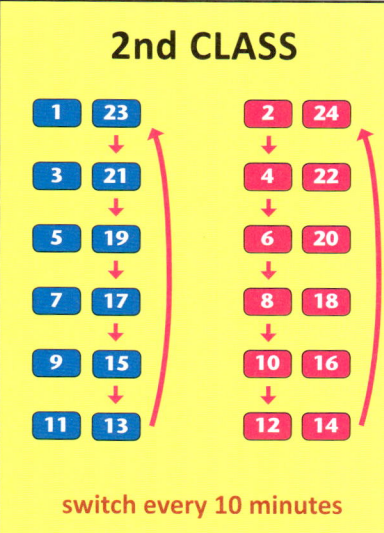

switch every 10 minutes

1. To ensure new partners, odds sit with odds and evens with evens.
2. You yell *Introduce yourself* and **SPEAK**!
3. After ten minutes, you yell **SWITCH**!

3rd CLASS

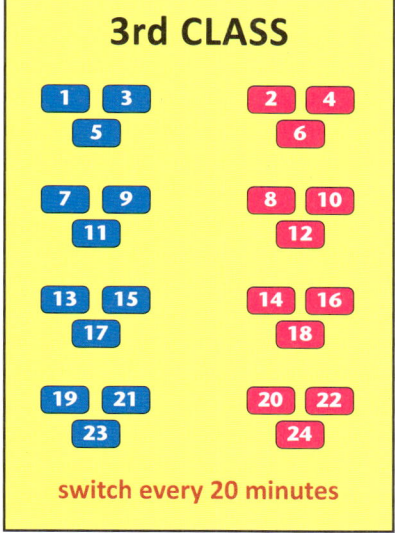

switch every 20 minutes

1. To ensure new partners and add variety, put students in threes.
2. You yell *Introduce yourself* and **SPEAK**!
3. After twenty minutes, you yell **SWITCH**!

REAL-WORLD ENGLISH

You're going to be having a lot of conversations.
Here are real-world comments and follow-up questions that keep conversations going.

TOP 20 COMMENT CATEGORIES

#	Category	Expressions
1.	Agree	Me too. I hear that. Ditto.
2.	Disagree	No way. Not me. When pigs fly. In your dreams.
3.	Change the topic	Anyway. By the way.
4.	Don't do that	Stop it. Cut it out. Knock it off!
5.	Hurry up	Chop chop. Cut to the chase. Shake a leg.
6.	I don't believe you	You're kidding. No way! Get real. Yeah, right. In your dreams. Say what?
7.	I don't care	Whatever.
8.	I don't understand	Excuse me? Again please. Say what?
9.	I want to also	I'm game. Count me in.
10.	I'm not sure	I have no idea. I have no clue. I have no earthly idea.
11.	Mistake	My bad. Oops. Uh-oh.
12.	Pain	Ouch! Eye yai yai.
13.	Privacy	No comment. That's personal. That's none of your business.
14.	Sarcasm	Hello? Anybody home? Du-uh. Like, du-uh.
15.	Surprise	What the heck!
16.	Sympathy	I'm sorry to hear that. That's a shame. That's terrible.
17.	That's too bad	Bummer. What a bummer. What a drag. Yuck!
18.	That's great	Wow! Awesome. No kidding! Cool. Neat. Congratulations.
19.	Whatever	Either way. Your call. Whatever suits you. I'll go with the flow.
20.	You're welcome	Don't mention it. Anytime. My pleasure.

FOLLOW-UP QUESTIONS

Where? When? Why? Who? How? How long? How often? What time?

And the greatest conversation question in the English language:

WHAT ABOUT YOU?

Sample Conversation

> **There are over 300 conversation-starting questions in this book.**
> You know the answer to every one because every question is about you.
>
> Today, RIGHT NOW, get in the habit of making comments and asking follow-up questions.
> This will make all your conversations longer. And more interesting, like you.

Brad	Hi. My name is Brad Kim.	
Britney	Hello, my name is Britney Lee. Nice to meet you.	
Brad	Nice to meet you, too. Say, aren't you also in my computer class?	
Britney	No, that must be my twin sister.	
Brad	No way! Really? Actually, I always wanted a twin. Just one of us would register for school and we could take turns going to class.	
Britney	I was kidding.	
Brad	Oh. Funny, ha ha. Anyway. Where do you live, Britney?	
Britney	I live just off campus, near the subway station. What about you?	
Brad	I live in Incheon, but I hope to move into the dormitory next semester. I hate spending three hours a day on the subway.	
Britney	I hear that. Will your grades be good enough to move into the dorm?	
Brad	No comment. Anyway, what did you do last weekend?	
Britney	I just hung out around school and met some of my classmates and went shopping. What about you?	
Brad	I hung around my house. I was going to study, but ended up sleeping most of the time.	
Britney	What's your major?	
Brad	I'm majoring in economics. And you?	
Britney	My major is French. Why did you choose economics?	
Brad	Originally, I wanted to major in business administration, but my father suggested economics.	
Britney	What does your father do?	
Brad	He's a banker.	
Britney	Well, that makes sense.	
Brad	What about you? Why did you choose French?	
Britney	I was born and raised in France and I lived there until I was 10. So I picked the easiest major possible.	
Brad	Lucky you. Say what? Class is over? Bummer. This was fun. It was nice to meet you.	
Britney	Nice meeting you, too. What are you doing after class?	
Brad	I have a class next period. In fact, I have three more classes back to back. And you?	
Britney	I'm going shopping with my twin brother. OK, well, I'll see you next week, same time, same place.	
Brad	Great. See you later. Wait. Twin? You said. . .	
Britney	Bye byeee e e	

FIRST-DAY SPEED DATING!

But we are total strangers. Exactly!
You'll switch partners every five minutes and meet a new stranger.

A conversation is like a butterfly. It can go anywhere.

Where do you live?
How long have you lived there? Where is your hometown?

How do you get to school?
How long does it take? Do you have a driver's license?

What did you do last night?
Where? How long did you stay? What time did you get home?

How many text messages do you send per day?
How many do you get? Who do you send the most to?

Who is your favorite English-language movie star?
Who is your favorite male star? Female star? Foreign star?

Are you a couch potato? (Do you watch TV all the time?)
Do you ever exercise? Are you glued to the sofa on Sunday?

How many people are there in your family?
Are you the first, middle, last or what? What does your father do?

Have you ever been very sick or in the hospital?
Why? When? For how long? What happened?

Do you look more like your father or mother?
How exactly? Are you taller than your father? Your mother?

What does your father do? What exactly does he do?
Is he a workaholic? Does he work much at home?

What will you do tonight? What time do you finish class?
Do you socialize around school, at home, or in your neighborhood?

Are you skilled at anything? Music, art, sports, sleeping?
Have you ever won a contest? Gotten a scholarship? Olympic medal?

What is your major? Did your parents help you choose it?
Why did you choose it? Do you have a minor yet?

How often do you go to a coffee shop?
How much coffee do you drink every day? Do you drink coffee to study?

How many universities did you apply to?
What school was your first choice? Did you stay out a year to study?

Are you a morning person or an evening person?
What time do you usually wake up? When do you study?

How often do you exercise? What exercise?
Do you use the weekends to study or hang out with your friends?

What do you usually do on the weekends?
Do you belong to a health club? How long do you exercise?

Who is your favorite singer or group?
Who's your favorite member? Can you sing? Dance?

Do you prefer the summer or the winter?
Why? What do you usually do during the summer / winter break?

How many hours do you sleep every night?
What time do you usually go to bed? Do you eat late at night?

What kind of books do you like to read?
On the subway, do you read, watch people, text, or play a game?

How many courses are you taking this semester?
What is your most difficult class? What is your busiest day?

Do you also go to an academy or institute?
What time do you go before or after school? How often do you go?

Are you close to your brother (or sister)?
Do you confide in them, or keep secrets? What is the age gap?

Which is more fun, high school or college?
Why, exactly? Do you still see any middle school friends?

Really? Say what? No kidding. No way! Get outta town! Me too. Bummer. Sort of. Sometimes. Half and half. It depends.
Who? Where? When? Why? What time? How long? How often? WHAT ABOUT YOU?

Sit face-to-face with your partner. Turn your book sideways. Your partner's book is closed.

Meet, greet, introduce yourself, ask any question, make comments, have a conversation.

Say goodbye. Change partners. Meet, greet, introduce yourself, ask any question, have a conversation.

Say goodbye. Change partners. Meet, greet, introduce yourself, ask any question, have a conversation.

A conversation is like a butterfly. *It can go anywhere.*

What high school did you go to?
What was your favorite subject in high school? Your least favorite?

Where were you born?
How long have you lived there? Did your family move many times?

What did you do last summer / winter vacation?
How long did you stay? Who did you go with? Would you go again?

Do any of your grandparents live with you?
On your mother or father's side? How often do you see them?

Do your parents give you an allowance?
How much? Is it enough? Do you get money on your birthday?

What will you do this weekend? On Saturday or Sunday?
Who will you go with? Will you clean your room?

What time is your curfew (when you must be home at night)?
What is the latest that you ever got home? Were you punished?

What is your favorite sport or exercise?
Do you like to play sports, or just watch them?

Have you ever fallen asleep and missed your subway or bus stop?
How long ago was that? How often does that happen?

What was your easiest subject last semester?
What is your hardest subject? Do you have a free day?

Are you good with computers?
What programs do you know? What is your favorite computer game?

How many hours per week are you taking this semester?
When is your busiest day? How many hours per day do you study?

Do you play a musical instrument?
How long have you played? How old were you when you started?

What did you do last weekend? *Who did you go with?*
Did you meet any high school friends?

Have you ever had a part-time job?
How often did you work? Where? When? How often?

What is your favorite TV show?
When does it come on? Who are the stars?

Do you have a hobby?
When did you start? How many do you have? How do you relax?

How long does it take you to get to school?
What time do you leave and get home? How do you get to school?

How many cell phones have you had in your life?
Did you lose any? Did you ever use one in an emergency?

What is your favorite Western food?
Do you prefer Chinese or Japanese food? Do you cook?

Who is more strict, your father or mother?
Do you get punished often? What was your worst punishment?

Does your mother work?
How long has she worked? Do you look like your mother or father?

What is your busiest day this semester?
How many classes do you have on Monday? Tue, Wed, Thu, Fri?

Are you more like your father or mother?
Why? Do they have similar personalities? Are they opposites?

Do you belong to a club or organization?
How many people are in it? Where do you meet? Join?

Who is your favorite movie star? Male star? Female star?
How often do you watch English movies? Where, usually?

Really? Say what? No kidding. No way! Get outta town! Me too. Bummer. Sort of. Sometimes. Half and half. It depends.
Who? Where? When? Why? What time? How long? How often? WHAT ABOUT YOU?

13

CLASSROOM MT

Meeting, Greeting, Inviting Out, Accepting, & Rejecting *Ugh!*

Introduce yourself to seven different people, and make a date for every day of the week.

Example		
Who	Brad Kim	When 6:30
Where	Doosan Tower	
Phone	019 - 5842-7723	
Email	ibjammin@net.com	

Monday — Who / When / Where / Phone / Email

Tuesday — Who / When / Where / Phone / Email

Wednesday — Who / When / Where / Phone / Email

Thursday — Who / When / Where / Phone / Email

Friday — Who / When / Where / Phone / Email

Saturday — Who / When / Where / Phone / Email

Sunday — Who / When / Where / Phone / Email

movies   coffee shop   shopping   eating   drinking   rollerblading   performance

INVITING SOMEONE OUT  3

Would you like to do something on Wednesday?
Are you busy on Tuesday? Are you free on Monday?
Do you have any plans this weekend?

What time are you free? What time is convenient?
What time do you want to meet? What time is good?

Where do you want to meet? Where can we meet?
I'm not familiar with that area.
Where exactly? What about meeting at _____?

SAYING YES: SURE!

OK.   Cool.   Sure!   You bet!   Great!
I'd love to.   Let's do it.   Count me in.   I'm game.

SAYING NO: I'D LOVE TO, BUT...

I'm busy.   I already have plans.   I can't.
I'm busy on Wednesday. What about Friday?
I'm free on Tuesday. Is that OK for you?
Oh, gee, I'm sorry. Can I have a rain check?
(This means you really really want to go, but can't.)
Oh, gee. I can't. My grandmother is sick.
(This is a lie. It means you don't want to go with them.)

Do NOT LOOK at their calendar to see if they are free. ASK THEM!

INSTRUCTIONS

This activity will show you how to:

1. Introduce yourself and invite someone out
2. Politely say yes
3. Politely arrange a convenient time
4. Politely say no (honestly or with a white lie)

This is not a police interrogation. Do not ask "What's your name?"

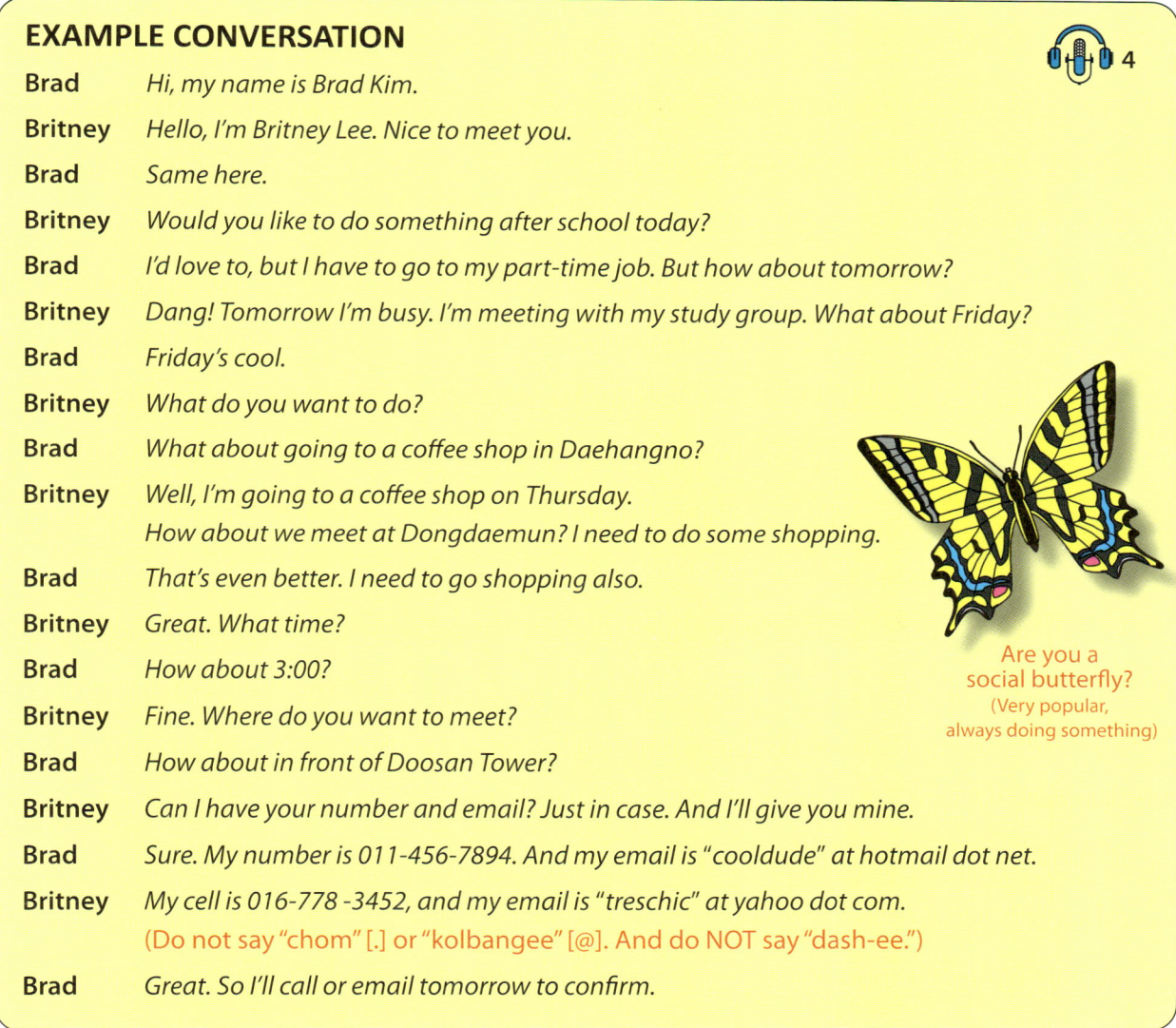

	EXAMPLE CONVERSATION
Brad	Hi, my name is Brad Kim.
Britney	Hello, I'm Britney Lee. Nice to meet you.
Brad	Same here.
Britney	Would you like to do something after school today?
Brad	I'd love to, but I have to go to my part-time job. But how about tomorrow?
Britney	Dang! Tomorrow I'm busy. I'm meeting with my study group. What about Friday?
Brad	Friday's cool.
Britney	What do you want to do?
Brad	What about going to a coffee shop in Daehangno?
Britney	Well, I'm going to a coffee shop on Thursday. How about we meet at Dongdaemun? I need to do some shopping.
Brad	That's even better. I need to go shopping also.
Britney	Great. What time?
Brad	How about 3:00?
Britney	Fine. Where do you want to meet?
Brad	How about in front of Doosan Tower?
Britney	Can I have your number and email? Just in case. And I'll give you mine.
Brad	Sure. My number is 011-456-7894. And my email is "cooldude" at hotmail dot net.
Britney	My cell is 016-778-3452, and my email is "treschic" at yahoo dot com. (Do not say "chom" [.] or "kolbangee" [@]. And do NOT say "dash-ee.")
Brad	Great. So I'll call or email tomorrow to confirm.

Are you a social butterfly?
(Very popular, always doing something)

This is not reading or writing class. It is conversation class.
DO NOT write your own information down. YOU say it, THEY write it. NOBODY reads.

If you have a **D**, **B**, or **P** in your address, the other person may not hear it correctly.
So you might have to say, *D as in dog, B as in boy, P as in puppy.*
The same for **M** and **N**. *Did you say M as in money? No, I said N as in no.*
The same for **Z** and **G**. *Was that Z as in zero or G as in go?*

PERSONALITY TEST

What kind of personality do you have?
Are you an exciting party animal or a studious party pooper?

🎧 5

#		Ex.	Me		Ex.	Me
1	Are you shy 수줍은	✓		or outgoing? 외향적인		
2	Are you a morning person 아침에 활동적인 사람	✓		or an evening person? 오후에 활동적인 사람		
3	Are you an indoor person 실내에서 활동하기를 좋아하는 사람	✓		or an outdoor person? 밖에서 활동하기 좋아하는 사람		
4	Are you a loner 혼자 있기를 좋아하는 사람	✓		or a joiner? 모임에 가입하거나 참여하기를 좋아하는 사람		
5	Are you neat 깔끔한, 정리정돈 잘하는	✓		or messy? 지저분한		
6	Are you punctual 시간을 잘 지키는	✓		or sometimes late? 지각하는, 늦는		
7	Does your father have patience 참을성 있는			or a short fuse? 참을성이 없어서 화를 쉽게 잘내는	✓	
8	Are you always polite 예의 바른			or sometimes rude? 무례한	✓	
9	Are you always on the go 활동적인	✓		or a couch potato? 게으르고 움직이기 싫어하는		
10	Is your father cheap 돈 쓰기에 인색한	✓		or a big spender? 돈을 잘쓰는		
11	Are you stingy 구두쇠인	✓		or generous? 베푸는		
12	Are you an early bird 아침 일찍 일어나고 부지런한 사람	✓		or a night owl? 밤늦게 활동하는 사람		
13	Are you a party pooper 파티를 망치는 사람			or a party animal? 파티를 좋아하는 사람, 파티광	✓	
14	Are you honest 있는 그대로 솔직히 말하는	✓		or do you tell white lies? 선한 거짓말을 하다		
15	Are your parents traditional 보수적인	✓		or modern? 현대적인		
16	Can you keep a secret 비밀을 지키는	✓		or are you a blabbermouth? 가십거리로 만들다/고자질하다	✓	
17	Are you well-organized 정리정돈을 매우 잘하는	✓		or do you often lose things? 정돈을 잘 못해서 물건을 자주 잃어버리는		
18	Are you modest 겸손한			or sometimes stuck-up? 잘난체하는/자만심이 강한	✓	
19	Are you a social drinker 사교를 위해 술 마시는 사람	✓		or a weekend warrior? 주말에 집중적으로 술을 마시는 사람		
20	Are your parents strict 엄격한	✓		or lenient? 관대한		

A high total here means you will be rich but a little bit boring. **16**

A high total here means you will be happy but not rich. **5**

**No kidding.   No way!   Say what?   Me too!   Bummer.   Kind of.
Sometimes.   Half and half.   It depends.   Why?   How, exactly?   For example?**

What about you?

INSTRUCTIONS

HOMEWORK: 1. Follow the examples. If you are shy, put a check in the box next to *shy*.
2. Add up how many checks you have in each column.

CLASSWORK: 1. Introduce yourself to your partner and give them a personality test.
2. If you are not totally honest, you can use "Kind of" or "It depends."
3. When your partner answers, "It depends," ask, "How, exactly?" or "For example?"

EXAMPLE CONVERSATION  6

Brad	*Hi, my name's Brad.*
Britney	*Hi, Brad, I'm Britney. Nice to meet you.*
Brad	*Same here.*
Britney	*I like your hat. It's, well, different.*
Brad	*Really? Thanks. I bought it in Myeong-dong. It was on sale for $2.*
Britney	*OK, I'll just put you down as a <u>big spender</u>.*
Brad	*Cool. Thanks.*
Britney	*I was joking. Two dollars is not much.*
Brad	*Oh. Anyway. So, are you <u>punctual</u> or sometimes <u>late</u>?*
Britney	*I'm never <u>late</u>. I think that being late is being <u>rude</u>.*
Brad	*Say what? You were <u>late</u> for class today.*
Britney	*Oh, yeah. About that. I stopped to help an old lady off the subway.*
Brad	*Oookay. I'll give you a check for <u>telling white lies</u>.*
Britney	*Helloooo. I was telling a <u>white lie</u> when I said I liked your hat.*
Brad	*Oh, wow. So you have a great personality and great beauty!*
Britney	*Thank you very much. That is so nice of you.*
Brad	*<u>White lie.</u>*
Britney	*Ah! Anyway. Are you a <u>morning person</u> or an <u>evening person</u>?*
Brad	*I'm an <u>evening person</u>. I hate to get up early. I rarely get up before 11.*
Britney	*Me too. What time do you usually go to bed?*
Brad	*Usually about 2 a.m. What about you?*
Britney	*I'm the same way.*
Brad	*OK, we're both evening people. What time do you go to bed on the weekends?*
Britney	*About the same time. And you?*
Brad	*On the weekends I stay up really late. Sometimes until sunrise.*
Britney	*What do you do when you stay up that late?*
Brad	*Usually I study English.*
Britney	*Really?*
Brad	*Gotcha!*

This activity only *pretends* to be an interview. If a conversation starts, go with it.

17

1 FAMILY

Scan and find the tracks.

Korean War veteran (and my uncle) Lee Broussard with his wife Jean, kids, and grandkids

 7

VOCABULARY VITAMINS

age gap	연령차	inherit, inheritance	상속하다, 상속
allowance	용돈, 수당	jealous	질투하는
ancestors	조상	military family	군인 가족
birth order	태어난 순서	musically inclined	음악적 성향이 있는
black sheep of the family	집안의 골치덩어리	only child	외동(딸,아들)
born and raised in	태어나서 자란 곳이	originally from	원래; 처음부터
close, close to	친하다	passed away	작고하시다
cousin / relative	사촌 / 친척	personal	사적인
curfew	통금시간	punish, punishment	벌하다
descendants	후손	quality time	가족과 함께 보내는 귀중한 시간
distant relative	먼 친척	religious family	종교적인 가족
divorce	이혼	scandal	추문
extended family	대가족	sibling	형제자매
family feud	가정 불화	spoiled, spoiled brat	버릇없는 아이
far-flung	멀리 사는	strict / lenient	엄격한 / 관대한
funeral / grave	장례식 / 무덤	supportive	지원하는; 도와주는
hometown	고향	take after; favor	(성격이) 닮다

Relatives

aunt	고모; 이모	maternal grandfather	외할아버지
aunt by marriage	숙모; 외숙모	maternal grandmother	외할머니
brother-in-law	매부; 처남	mother-in-law	장모; 시어머니
children	어린이	nephew	남자조카
father-in-law	장인; 시아버지	niece	여자조카
first cousin	친사촌	paternal grandfather	친할아버지
great-grandfather	증조부	paternal grandmother	친할머니
great-great-grandfather	고조부	sister-in-law	시누이; 처제, 올케
half-brother	부모가 재혼 후 낳은 남자 형제	stepbrother / sister	의붓형제 / 자매
half-sister	부모가 재혼 후 낳은 여자 형제	uncle	삼촌

CONVERSATION STARTERS

1. This is the dialog to your English life. Write what you will say, and talk about what you wrote.
2. This is NOT an interview. If a conversation starts, go with it. Conversation is KING.

1. **How many people are there in your family?** *Where were you born? Where do you live now?*
   There are five in my family: my grandmother, father, mother, my older sister, and me.

2. **Who's the oldest among your siblings?** *How old is your brother? Your sister?*
   I am the last of three children. My sister is 24. Our age gap is four years.

3. **Is your extended family big (aunt, uncles, cousins, everybody)?**
   Yes. I have four uncles and four aunts on both my mother's and father's sides.

4. **What does your father do?** *How long has he worked there?*
   My father is a high school math teacher in Mok-dong. He's worked there since forever.

5. **Does your mother work?** *What does she do?*
   Not anymore. She was a nurse before she got married. She's studying to be a real estate agent.

6. **What school or university do your brothers or sisters go to?**
   My older brother works for Samsung, and my younger sister goes to Yonsei.

7. **Are you close to your brother or sister?** *Who is smarter? Better-looking?*
   I'm close to my sister, but not my brother. He's eight years older than me.

8. **Are you more like [similar to] your father or mother?** *Looks? Personality? Build?*
   I think that I am more like my mother. We are both shy and artistic.

| Really? | No kidding! | No way! | Me too! | Kind of. | It depends. |

What about you?

CONVERSATION STARTERS  9

This is the dialog to your English life. Write what you will say, and talk about what you wrote.

9. **Are your parents strict?** *What time is your curfew? What was your worst punishment?*
   My father is usually strict, and my mother is very lenient. Once, they took away my phone for a month.
   _____

10. **Are you close to your grandparents?** *First cousins? Uncles or aunts?*
    I am close to my maternal grandmother. She used to babysit me when I was young.
    _____

11. **What does your family do on Sunday?** *What time do you wake up on Sunday?*
    We usually go to church, and then my father takes us to a nice restaurant.
    _____

12. **How many times has your family moved?** *Which place is your favorite? Why?*
    We have moved only once. I was born in Anyang, and we moved to Seoul when I was 10.
    _____

13. **Is your whole family talented in one area, like music, art, or math?**
    Yes, my whole family is pretty good at music. We all play an instrument. I play the violin.
    _____

14. **Do your parents give you an allowance?** *Have you ever had a part-time job?*
    Yes, they give me about 200,000 won a month. Sometimes more. I tutored a middle-school student.
    _____

15. **If it's not too personal, is your whole family the same religion?**
    No, that's OK. My mother and I are Christians, but my father has no religion.
    _____

16. **Have you ever told your parents a big lie?** *Do your parents like your friends?*
    Yes. Once, I went to visit my boyfriend, but I told my parents I went to the library.
    _____

Write your own question: *Does your family have a pet?*

Where? When? Who? Why? How long? How often? What about you?

MODEL CONVERSATION

At home, listen and repeat five times. Your pronunciation will DEFINITELY improve.

Brad	Hi. My name is Brad. (Don't say *What's your name?*)
Britney	Hi. My name is Britney. Nice to meet you.
Brad	You too. Is this your first class today?
Britney	No, I have a class first period. What about you?
Brad	This is my first. I'm not a <u>morning person</u>. Say, where are you from, Britney?
Britney	<u>Originally from</u> Atlanta. I was <u>born and raised</u> there. My family moved to California when I was 17.
Brad	Really? How many people are there in your family?
Britney	I'm the middle of three. I have an older brother and a younger sister. <u>What about you?</u>
Brad	I'm the youngest of four. I have three older sisters.
Britney	Aha, did your father keep trying for a son?
Brad	Yeah, I think that's what happened. The <u>age gap</u> between each of my sisters is about two years, and then between me and my next sister is six years.
Britney	I'll bet your grandparents love you!
Brad	Oh, yeah. I'm their only grandson. You should see the photos of my 100-day party.
Britney	I can imagine. Are you <u>close to</u> your sisters?
Brad	Not really. They're <u>close to</u> each other, but not so much to me.
Britney	Are they <u>jealous</u> of all the attention you get?
Brad	Not anymore. I think they gave up. Plus, I'm so darned cute.
Britney	[cough] Oh, yeah. Right. I see it now.

Quality time

Future *Jazz English* author

Who is the tallest in your family?	
tallest	
best-looking	ME
smartest	
funniest	
most athletic	
best singer	
best dresser	
cheapest	
biggest spender	
most religious	
heaviest drinker	
wakes up first	
goes to bed last	
watches TV the most	

TOP 5 CULTURAL DIFFERENCES

These cultural differences can also be conversation starters. You can ask:
What do you think about number 1? How do you feel about number 2? Which way do you prefer?

1. In Korea, wives usually must respect and obey their mother-in-law. In America, mothers-in-law have no power over their daughters-in-law.

2. In Korea the oldest son is expected to take care of his parents in their old age. Thus, some women would prefer not to marry the oldest son. This is not the case in America.

3. In Korea, wives generally control the money. In America it is generally the opposite or 50-50.

4. America has more interracial marriages than Korea. However, such marriages are increasing in Korea.

5. Koreans have a preference for boys, whereas Americans have no particular preference.

CULTURE QUESTIONS

*What would your parents say if you wanted to date a foreigner?
If your first child were a daughter, would you have two children?
Males, do you have one older sister? Females, do you have one younger brother?*

VOCABULARY DEVELOPMENT

To master a new vocabulary word, you must use it several times in several ways.
All the answers are in the VOCABULARY VITAMINS on page 18.

ACROSS

1. Your mother's mother is your _____ grandmother.
5. If parents are too lenient, a child may be _____.
6. If your parents punish you for not making an A+, they are probably very _____.
8. Your great-grandparents are your _____.
9. Your brother or sister's daughter is your _____.
11. Your brother or sister's son is your _____.
12. Your father or mother's sister is your _____.
13. Your father or mother's brother is your _____.

DOWN

2. Money from your parents every week
3. Your uncle and aunt's children are your _____.
4. If a husband and wife hate each other, they sometimes get a _____.
7. The opposite of strict is _____.
10. If your family does a lot of things together, your family is _____.

LONGER & SMOOTHER SPEAKING

This will help you speak longer and more smoothly. Try to use some Vocabulary Vitamins.
Write what you will say, and talk about what you wrote.

WRITE ABOUT YOUR FAMILY
Jobs, majors, hobbies, looks, personality, where you have lived, whatever.

There are six people in my family: my father, mother, two older sisters, one younger brother, and me. I was born and raised in Gwangju, and we moved to Seoul right before I started college. My father is a principal at a private high school, and my mother is a housewife. My parents are the outdoor type. Every morning they play badminton, and every weekend they go hiking in the mountains. We are all close, and we always take vacations together. My whole family is musically inclined. We all play at least one musical instrument. In fact, my mother used to be a piano teacher until she got married.

My oldest sister is married and she's a pharmacist. She has a son and a daughter. My other sister is a university senior majoring in chemistry at Hanyang University. She wants to go to graduate school and be a professor. My younger brother is a senior in high school, and he's preparing for his college entrance exams. I'm a sophomore English major at Kyung Hee University. I'm an outgoing, outdoor, evening person, and my hobby is playing tennis. I play about twice a week.

You could type it on a computer and tape it above. This would check your spelling and grammar! Cool.

CONVERSATION

HOMEWORK:
1. **Try to create your own question.** For example, look at the first one: *What time do you go to bed?*
2. Then look at the questions at the bottom to see if yours is correct. If it's not correct, fix it.
3. Put a question in EVERY top blank. (You can scratch out a question after you use it.)

1	Goes to bed at the same time as you	6	Wakes up at the same time as you
	What time do you go to bed?		
	Kim Mee-soo		
2	Is in the same birth order	7	Has the same number of aunts
3	Has the same number of brothers	8	Is the same height as you
			How tall are you?
			rlzkim25tel@netmail.com
4	Has the same number of nieces	9	Lives in a dormitory
5	Has a grandparent living with them	10	Has the same family size

1. Do any grandparents live with you?	6. How many brothers do you have?
2. Do you have an older brother?	7. How many in your family?
3. Do you have your own bedroom?	8. How many nieces do you have?
4. Do you live in the dormitory?	9. How many sisters do you have?
5. How many aunts do you have?	10. How many uncles do you have?

Questions

Really?   **No kidding!**   **No way!**   **Me too!**   **Say what?**   **Bummer.**

What about you?

STATION

CLASSWORK: Speed date in pairs, or have longer three-person conversations, or meet and mingle.

1. Ask your partner a question. If your partner has the same answer as you, write down their name. If you know their name, write down their email address. (This will help <u>their</u> pronunciation and <u>your</u> listening.)
2. If you had no time to do the homework (bummer), just ask your partner the questions at the bottom.
3. *Remember, conversation is KING. If a conversation starts, go with it.*

11	Father has the same job as yours	16	Has the same number of sisters
12	Curfew is at the same time as yours	17	Gets home at the same time after school
13	Mother is the same age as yours	18	Father is the same age as yours
14	Has the same number of uncles	19	Has an older brother
15	Has their own bedroom	20	Has the same hobby

Questions

11. How old is your father?
12. How old is your mother?
13. ~~How tall are you?~~
14. What does your father do?
15. What is your hobby?
16. What time do you get home after school?
17. ~~What time do you go to bed?~~
18. What time do you wake up?
19. What time is your curfew?
20. Where are you in the birth order?

Where?   When?   Why?   Who?   How?   What time?   How often?

What about you?

25

2 HOBBIES & INTERESTS

USEFUL EXPRESSIONS

HOW LONG HAVE YOU ...?
I began playing when I was 10. = I have played since I was 10.
I began playing in 2010. = I have played since 2010.
I started playing when I was in elementary school.

I have been playing for ten years. = I have played for ten years.
I have been playing since I was in middle school.

HOW OFTEN DO YOU ...?
I play once · twice · three · four times a week.
I play every other day · every other weekend.

USED TO
I <u>used to</u> play, but not anymore.
I <u>used to play</u> in middle school, but then I stopped.
I stopped taekwondo when I started high school.

ABILITY
If someone asks if you are good at your hobby, you can answer *yes*, *no*, or *so-so*.

Or you can be more specific:
Are you good at tennis?
I'm bad / pretty bad.
I'm not too good.
I'm OK. I'm so-so. Not really.
I'm pretty good. I'm very good.
I'm good! I'm an expert.

WOW!
If someone is really good, do not say, *I envy you*.
Americans do not say that.
They say, *Wow!*

 12

VOCABULARY VITAMINS

HOBBIES

aerobics	에어로빅	golf	골프	ping pong	탁구
astronomy	천문학	hiking	도보여행	singing	노래부르기
badminton	배드민턴	martial arts	무술	soccer	축구
bicycle riding	자전거 타기	mountain hiking	등산	sports	스포츠
bowling	볼링	musical instrument	악기	surfing the Internet	인터넷 서핑
calligraphy	서예	painting	(물감으로 그린) 그림	swimming	수영
camping	캠핑	photography	사진	tennis	테니스
computer games	컴퓨터 게임	reading	독서	yoga, Pilates	요가, 필라테스
cooking	요리	rollerblading	롤러블레이딩	**COLLECTING**	수집
crossword puzzles	크로스워드 퍼즐	scuba diving	스쿠바 다이빙	coins	동전수집
drawing	그림, 데생	sewing	바느질하기	dolls	인형수집
fishing	낚시	shooting pool	당구	stamps	우표수집

 13 **CONVERSATION STARTERS**

You use this page; your partner will use page B. Or vice-versa.
Ask any question you like (at random) and ask FOLLOW-UP QUESTIONS. (Where? When? Why?)

1. **Do you have a hobby? (NOT *Are you have a hobby?*) *How often do you ...?***
   My hobby is rollerblading. I rollerblade along the Han River about twice a week.

   _____

2. **How long have you had your hobby? *Are you any good at it?***
   I started playing tennis when I was about 10. I used to collect stamps, but I don't anymore.

   _____

3. **Do you belong to a club or organization? *Is it a school club? A club in your major?***
   I belong to a photography club. We have about twenty members.

   _____

4. **What do you usually do on the weekends? *Are you an indoors or outdoors person?***
   I just relax around the house and play with my kids. Or I catch up on my work.

   _____

5. **Does your mother or father have a hobby? *How often do they do it?***
   My parents play badminton every morning. They have cute matching uniforms, like a campus couple.

   _____

6. **Are you taking any elective courses? *Something that interests you?***
   Yeah, I'm taking a photography course. That could be my new hobby if I have the time and money.

   _____

7. **Are you very talented in anything—athletic, artistic, musical?**
   I'm not. My older brother is good at sports, and my younger sister plays the piano.

   _____

8. **Do you ever exercise or play any sports? *Do you prefer to play or watch a sport?***
   I don't like to sweat, but sometimes I ride my bike along the Han River. I like watching soccer.

   _____

Really?   No kidding!   No way!   Me too!   Kind of.   Half and half.   It depends.

What about you?

B CONVERSATION STARTERS

Write what you will say, and talk about what you wrote.

9. **Have you ever collected anything?** *Have you ever won a contest? Athletic? Science project?*
   For a while I collected money from different countries. Oh, I won a science project in the sixth grade.
   _____

10. **How often do you exercise?** *How often do you sleep until noon?*
    I play badminton every other day, and I go to the health club twice a week.
    _____

11. **Do you like to cook?** *How often do you cook? Do you cook for anyone else?*
    Yes. My mother works, so I often cook for my family.
    _____

12. **What is your favorite computer game?** *How often do you play?*
    I like League of Legends. I play it every chance I get. Once, I played for ten hours nonstop.
    _____

13. **Is it more relaxing to do something or nothing?**
    Oh, I could do nothing for a long, long time. On Sunday I watch TV for about eight hours.
    _____

14. **What kind of books do you like to read?** *Where do you get your news? TV? Newspaper?*
    I used to read a lot of comic books, but now I like historical novels.
    _____

15. **Have you ever traveled abroad?** (NOT *to abroad*) *How long did you stay?*
    Yes, I have been to Japan and China. I stayed for about five days in each country.
    _____

16. **When's the last time that you went to a museum, art gallery, or concert?**
    Let's see. I went to an opera at the Performing Arts Center last month.
    _____

Write your own question: *Do you collect anything? Stamps? Hats?*

| Where? | When? | Why? | How long? | How often? | How many? |

What about you?

 15

MODEL CONVERSATION

At home, listen and repeat five times. Your pronunciation will DEFINITELY improve.

Brad Hey, Britney! Long time no see.
Britney Yeah. Did you finish the homework? It was hard.
Brad Homework?
Britney Just kidding.
Brad Funny, ha ha. So, Britney, do you have a hobby?
Britney Yes, I like to go rollerblading.
Brad Where do you go?
Britney My sister and I go rollerblading along the Han River near Hanyang University.
Brad Neat. How often do you go?
Britney We go every weekend, usually on Saturday afternoon. What about you?
Brad My hobby is soccer. I'm on my department's soccer team here at school.
Britney What position do you play?
Brad Well, I used to be the goalie, but last game we lost 8 to 0, so now I just kind of run around and yell.
Britney Bummer.
Brad That's OK; I need the exercise. How long have you been rollerblading? Are you any good?
Britney I started in middle school. I'm OK. Now I'm working on going backwards.
Brad Do you wear all those fancy pads and a helmet and stuff?
Britney Absolutely. Looking good is half the fun. What's your favorite soccer team?
Brad Manchester United. People tell me I look like a young Cristiano Ronaldo.
Britney [cough] Oh, yeah. I see it now.

The taekwondo dojang in my neighborhood. He's not a wannabe; he's the real deal: a fifth-degree black belt.

TOP 5 CULTURAL DIFFERENCES

These cultural differences can also be conversation starters. You can ask:
What do you think about number 1? How do you feel about number 2? Which way do you prefer?

1. A hobby is an activity, something you *do*. Americans do not consider "watching movies" or "listening to music" a hobby.

2. An American's hobby is likely to be an individual activity, whereas in Korea it is probably a group activity.

3. Classical music is more popular in Korea, so more people have music as a hobby. Koreans are more likely to play a musical instrument than Americans are.

4. Because many Americans are overweight, many hobbies involve exercise activities.

5. Team sports in leagues are a common hobby in America.

CULTURE QUESTION
Do you prefer team or individual sports or activities? Why?

She was one of my students, but her makeup was so thick I couldn't figure out which one.

> You could say that a hobby is something you could make money doing if you were very good at it.
> For example, *tennis, playing the piano, photography, carpentry, painting, sewing.*
> People don't get paid just to watch movies or listen to music. (NOT *the music*)

VOCABULARY DEVELOPMENT

To master a new vocabulary word, you must use it several times in several ways.
All the answers are in the VOCABULARY VITAMINS on page 26.

ACROSS
2. How often do you _____ the Internet?
5. You change your shoes to do this.
8. My father likes mountain _____.
9. You use a racquet but not a ball.
12. You use a racquet and a furry ball.
13. The lowest score wins.

DOWN
1. I like _____ things, such as stamps and coins.
3. My father likes _____. He collects rare books.
4. This is good for meditation and stretching.
6. This is a good hobby for your heart and lungs.
7. I like to take _____ with my iPhone.
10. I'm no Picasso, but I like _____.
11. I like to _____ but there is no pool near my house. (NOT *near to my house*)

LONGER & SMOOTHER SPEAKING

This will help you speak longer and more smoothly. Try to use some Vocabulary Vitamins.
Write what you will say, and talk about what you wrote.

WRITE ABOUT YOUR HOBBY AND INTERESTS
You can include details, such as where, when, with whom,
how long you've been doing it, how often, how many.

My hobby is taekwondo, and I belong to the club here at school. I started taking taekwondo in the first grade, so I have been practicing for twelve years. I'm a fourth-degree black belt. In high school I was on the demonstration team. That was a lot of hard work, but we won some contests and I have some trophies. Our university club meets <u>once a week</u>, but I wish we met more often. If you meet less than <u>three times a week</u> you don't improve. I like taekwondo because it keeps me physically fit, and I get a <u>sense of satisfaction</u> that I am very good at something. Also, it is <u>rewarding</u> to help the younger kids learn. Taekwondo is kind of a team sport in that you practice with a group, but it is also an individual sport in that you compete by yourself.

My parents' hobby is badminton. They belong to a league at our local health club. They play about twice a week in the mornings before work. They have matching uniforms, and they look like a campus couple. They are really <u>into</u> badminton. My mother also teaches bible study to children at our church. That gives her a <u>sense of fulfillment</u>. She likes helping people.

You could type it on a computer and tape it above. This would check your spelling and grammar! Cool.

CONVERSATION

HOMEWORK:
1. **Try to create your own question.** For example, look at the first one: *Do you belong to a club?*
2. Then look at the questions at the bottom to see if yours is correct. If it's not correct, fix it.
3. Put a question in EVERY top blank. (You can scratch out a question after you use it.)

1	Belongs to a club	6	Goes bowling (NOT *plays*)
	Do you belong to a club? *Park Min-soo*		
2	Plays badminton	7	Draws or paints
3	Enjoys photography	8	Plays a musical instrument
4	Goes rollerblading	9	Likes to cook
5	Is a good swimmer	10	Is a couch potato
			Are you a couch potato? *napking@netmail.com*

1. ~~Are you a couch potato?~~
2. Are you a good swimmer?
3. Can you draw or paint?
4. Do you do volunteer work?
5. Do you collect anything?

Questions

6. ~~Do you belong to a club?~~
7. Do you like to cook?
8. Do you help at your church?
9. Do you ever go bowling? (NOT *play*)
10. Do you ever play badminton?

Really?   No kidding!   No way!   Me too!   Say what?   Bummer.

What about you?

CLASSWORK: Speed date in pairs, or have longer three-person conversations, or meet and mingle.

1. Ask your partner a question. If your partner has the same answer as you, write down their name.
   If you know their name, write down their email address. (This will help <u>their</u> pronunciation and <u>your</u> listening.)
2. If you had no time to do the homework (bummer) just ask your partner the questions at the bottom.
3. **Remember, conversation is KING. If a conversation starts, go with it.**

11	Plays a sport	16	Collects something
12	Plays a computer game	17	Does volunteer work
13	Has won an athletic event	18	Sleeps till noon
14	Helps at their church	19	Does aerobics
15	Takes taekwondo	20	Watches a lot of movies

11. Do you ever go rollerblading?
12. Do you ever sleep till noon?
13. Do you like to take pictures?
14. Do you play a sport?
15. Do you play a musical instrument?

Questions

16. Do you do aerobics?
17. Do you take taekwondo?
18. Have you ever won an athletic event?
19. How many movies do you watch per week?
20. Do you play a computer game?

Where?   When?   Why?   Who?   How?   What time?   How often?

What about you?

33

3 UNIVERSITY

Scan and find the tracks.

 17

VOCABULARY VITAMINS

TOP TEN PERSONALITY OPPOSITES

brainiac	머리가 매우 좋은	slow learner	인지능력이 부족해서 습득이 느린
easy grader	점수 후하게 주는 교수님	hard grader	점수를 깐깐하게 주는 교수님
geek; nerd	오로지 한가지만 잘하는 얼간이	jock	학업보다 운동에 열중하는 학생
idea person	아이디어가 많고 창의적인	detail person	꼼꼼하게 일하는 사람
joiner	모임에 가입하기 좋아하는 사람	loner	혼자있기를 좋아하는 사람
lenient; easygoing	관대한	strict	엄격한
long attention span	장시간 집중력	short attention span	짧은 집중력
party animal	학구적인, 공부벌레	party pooper	분위기를 깨는 사람
studious; bookworm	학구적인, 공부벌레	slacker	학업을 게을리하고 놀기만 하는 사람
underachiever	학업능률이 낮은 학생	overachiever	학업 능률이 높은 학생

alumni, alumnus	동문	post the grades	성적을 공개하다
apply, application	지원하다	procrastinate	미루다
apply yourself	최선을 다해 노력하다	pull an all-nighter	밤새 공부하다
bookstore	서점	recharge my batteries	재충전하다
cafeteria	학교 식당	roll sheet (attendance)	출석부
cheat sheet	컨닝 페이퍼	register	등록하다
clique	패거리	scholarship	장학금
coed	남녀공학	semester break	방학
college; university	대학	skip class; play hooky	수업 빼먹다
courses; classes; subjects	과목	syllabus	강의 계획서
cram	벼락치기	stay out	휴학
credits; hours	학점	transfer	편입하다
curriculum	교육과정	tuition	수업료
dean	학장	boarding house	하숙집
degree	학위	commute	통학하다
dictionary	사전	dormitory, dorm	기숙사
double major	복수전공	off campus	대학 캠퍼스 밖에 있는
drop-add period	수강신청 변경기간	walking distance	걸어서 갈수 있는 가까운 거리
exchange student	교환학생	major / minor	전공/부전공
excused absence	정당한 결석	required / elective	필수과목/선택과목
flunk; fail	낙제하다	freshman: 1학년	sophomore: 2학년
grades	성적	junior: 3학년	senior: 4학년
medical excuse	건강상의 이유로 결석	undergrad(uate)	학부생
midterms; midterm exams NOT middle term exams		graduate (grad) student	대학원생

CONVERSATION STARTERS

Each question is designed to start a conversation. If a conversation starts, GO WITH IT.

1. **What year are you?** *What is your major? Do you like your major?*
   I am a freshman and my major is design. I will specialize in fashion design my junior year.

2. **How many hours are you taking this semester?** *How many courses?*
   I am taking twenty hours. Seven classes: three major courses, two required, and one elective course.

3. **Have you ever gotten a scholarship?** *Were you ever a class leader?*
   Yes. I got a scholarship after my first semester. My parents were very proud.

4. **Do you belong to a club or study group?** *How often does it meet?*
   Both. I belong to a computer circle and to an English study group.

5. **Do you cram for exams?** *Do you study at home or in the library?*
   Yes. I never study until the last minute. But this semester I will try harder!

6. **Do you use the weekends to recharge your batteries or study?**
   Half and half. On Saturdays I goof off, and on Sunday afternoons I start getting ready for the week.

7. **Did you go to an all-girls or all-boys middle and high school?** *Where?*
   Yes. I went to an all-girls middle and high school in Anyang. In high school I lived in a dormitory.

8. **How many universities did you apply to?** *Is this your first choice? (Last choice?)*
   I applied to four universities and this was my second choice, but I am really happy here.

Really?   You're kidding.   No way.   Me too!   Say what?   Bummer.
Where?   When?   Why?   Who?   What time?   How?   How long?   How often?
Kind of.   Sometimes.   Half and half.   It depends.

What about you?

35

CONVERSATION STARTERS

9. **Do you have a part-time job?** *What did you do last summer / winter vacation?*
   I had a part-time job last semester, but I quit to concentrate on school.

10. **Do you have a free day?** *What do you do? What is your busiest day?*
    Yes, my free day is Monday. I clean my room and study. Just kidding. I sleep and watch TV.

11. **Has your cell phone ever rung in a class?** *Have you ever fallen asleep in class?*
    No, I always turn my cell phone off, but in high school I used to fall asleep all the time.

12. **Have you ever taken an online course?** *Are they easy? Were you ever absent? (Joke.)*
    I tried taking an online course but I dropped it. I don't have the self-discipline to work alone.

13. **How many hours do you study per day?** *Where? What time?*
    I study about two hours per day in the school library before going home. Usually. Well, sometimes.

14. **How do you get to school?** *How long does it usually take? Are you ever late for class?*
    I take the subway from Incheon. Oh, I hate that. It's an hour and a half each way.

15. **Are you a transfer student?** *Would you like to transfer?*
    I plan on taking a year off from classes and studying so that I can transfer to another school.

16. **Which is more fun, high school or college?** *Why? For example?*
    Definitely college. My freshman year I missed my high school friends, but not anymore.

Write your own question: _____

> *Really?* *You're kidding.* *No way.* *Me too!* *Say what?* *Bummer.*
> *Where? When? Why? Who? What time? How? How long? How often?*
> *Kind of.* *Sometimes.* *Half and half.* *It depends.*

MODEL CONVERSATION

Brad   Wow, Britney, long time no see.

Britney   Yeah, how are you, Brad?

Brad   Tired. Today is my busy day. I have classes from 9:00 to 3:00 nonstop.

Britney   Ouch.

Brad   Yeah, I'm starving. What's your schedule like this semester?

Britney   I'm taking twenty hours, but I'm thinking of <u>dropping a course</u>. I have only one class on Tuesday and it's an elective, so I might drop it.

Brad   What class?

Britney   It's a beginner course in computer programming, but I just don't get it. I'm not a <u>detail person</u>.

Brad   I know what you mean.

Britney   So, how's the rest of your schedule?

Brad   Great. I have late morning and early afternoon classes on Wednesday and Thursday, and I finish at 6:00 on Friday. Just in time to party.

Britney   Party? How were your grades last semester?

Brad   No comment. It was a conspiracy. All my teachers were <u>hard graders</u>.

Britney   Really. Wait, didn't you <u>flunk</u> a class because you were absent too many times?

Brad   Anyway. This semester I'm going to <u>apply myself</u> and make straight As.

Britney   In your dreams. Did you EVER make an A in college?

Brad   Well, excuse me for not being a <u>brainiac</u> like you.

Britney   I'm not a brainiac; I just <u>keep up with</u> my homework. You <u>goof off</u> all week, party all weekend, and try to <u>cram</u> on Sunday night.

Brad   Fine. Next topic. Do you still live in the <u>dormitory</u>?

Britney   Yeah, it's really convenient. I hated the <u>commute</u> to Incheon. And my roommate is from France, and she's really good at English.

Brad   Is she cute?

The bad news is, she fell asleep. The good news is, she came to class even though she was tired, so no points off.

What is your _____ class?
favorite
easiest
hardest
biggest
smallest
earliest

What is your _____ day?
longest
shortest
free

TOP 6 CULTURAL DIFFERENCES

These cultural differences can also be conversation starters. You can ask:
What do you think about number 1? How do you feel about number 2? Which way do you prefer?

1. In Korea, high school is very, very difficult, and university is easier. America is the opposite. High school is easy, and university is difficult. Graduate school is very difficult.

2. In general, American university students take fewer hours (15 to 18) per semester than Koreans, but study more. Korean students take more hours (18 to 21) and study less.

3. American students don't have to choose a major until their second year. And often they change their major more than once.

Short attention span

4. The average age at Korean universities is about 21, but in America it is about 24. Students may be people who quit their jobs to get another degree, or they may keep their jobs and go to school part-time. These "adult" students are in their 40s, 50s, and even older.

5. American high schools have four years, just like universities. Thus, students in both high school and college are called *freshmen, sophomores, juniors,* and *seniors*.

6. Korean universities have class leaders, and Korean students often go on Membership Training (MT). American universities do not have MT.

CULTURE QUESTIONS

Can you name some differences between Korean and American professors?
Would you prefer to have a foreign English professor or a Korean professor? Give three reasons why.
Have you ever lied to a foreign teacher, hoping they did not know Korean culture and would believe you?

VOCABULARY DEVELOPMENT

ACROSS

2. That _____ better start studying or he'll flunk out.
3. She's a _____. Straight As and never studies.
4. My scholarship pays for _____ and books.
5. I have a short _____ span. The longest I ever studied was 45 minutes. My goal is an hour.
8. My professor is too _____. I was ten minutes late and he marked me absent.
10. The _____ says homework is 50% of the grade.
11. How many schools did you _____ to?
12. Will you _____ online or go to school?

DOWN

1. I lost my _____ because of my low grades.
3. This weekend I'll rest and recharge my _____.
6. I'm going to stay out of school next _____.
7. What did you do during the semester _____?
9. I'm going to party now and _____ Sunday night.

LONGER & SMOOTHER SPEAKING

YOUR CHOICE. DESCRIBE YOUR:
(1) university personality, or (2) three most important classes, or (3) class schedule

Write about what you want to talk about.

(1) College life is rough. In high school I could goof off and <u>procrastinate</u> all week and just <u>cram</u> the night before a test, and still make good grades. In those days, I wasn't an <u>overachiever</u>, but my grades were above average. These days, I'm studying harder, and I feel like such an <u>underachiever</u>. In college, the courses are harder, the teachers are <u>stricter</u>, and the grading is harder. There are a bunch of <u>brainiacs</u> in my class and they all have their own <u>clique</u>. (And so on.)

(2) This semester my most important class is French Culture. My major is French, and it's important to learn French culture because language and culture are closely related. We are learning French history, and after the midterm we will read some French novels and see some French movies. I like history and movies, so that's great. The good news is the professor is French; the bad news is she assigns a lot of homework. (And so on.)

(3) This semester I'm taking twenty hours, seven courses total. Three are major courses, two required courses, and two elective courses. (And so on.)

You could type it on a computer and tape it above. This would check your spelling and grammar! Cool.

Conversation Station

1. You can roll the die, and if it lands with 2 facing up, ask any 2 question.
2. Ask a 1 question, and after everyone answers, ask a 2 question. Then a 3, 4, 5, and 6.
3. Ask the first 1 question, then the second, then the third, and fourth.

But first, current events! If you are meeting someone for the first time, take care of the basics:
Hi. My name is. . . .   Where do you live?   What is your major?   What high school did you go to?

Do you ...?
1. Cram or prepare ahead of time?
2. Procrastinate until the last minute?
3. Do your homework just before class?
4. Have a part-time job?
5. Take the subway to school?

Are you ...?
1. A party animal or party pooper?
2. An idea person or a detail person?
3. A joiner or a loner?
4. An underachiever or overachiever?
5. A brainiac or slow learner?

Have you ever ...?
1. Dropped a course? Which class? Why?
2. Gotten a scholarship?
3. Stayed out of school a year?
4. Bought a present for Teacher's Day?
5. Fallen asleep in class?

How many ...?
1. Hours are you taking?
2. Courses are you taking?
3. A+s will you get this semester?
4. Free days do you have?
5. Female professors do you have?

What time ...?
1. Do you usually wake up? Go to bed?
2. Is your earliest class? Latest class?
3. Is your best time to study?
4. Will you leave school today?
5. Do you usually eat lunch?

How often do you ...?
1. Complain about a score or grade?
2. Get the highest grade in class?
3. Get to class late?
4. Lie about your missing homework?
5. Drink coffee? Beer? Soju? Study?

 Remember, conversation is KING. If a conversation starts, go with it.

Really?   You're kidding.   No way.   Me too!   Say what?   Bummer.
Where?   When?   Why?   Who?   What time?   How?   How long?   How often?
Kind of.   Sometimes.   Half and half.   It depends.

What about you?

UNIVERSITY FREQUENCY

HOMEWORK: Fill in the blanks with your answers. For example, look at question 1.
If you exercise three times a week, give yourself an 8. Fill in all the blanks in the second column and then add them up.

CLASSWORK: You and your partner will interview each other. When you answer, try to use a phrase in regular type and a phrase in italics. But if a conversation starts, GO with it.

Brad	*How often do you study for three hours nonstop?*	
Britney	*As often as possible. Three times a week.*	
Brad	*Really? No kidding? That's pretty good.*	
Britney	*What about you?*	
Brad	*Very frequently. Every day.*	**EXAMPLE**
Britney	*Yeah, and I'm Jeon Ji-hyun.*	**CONVERSATION**

HOW OFTEN DO YOU ...?

	Ex	ME
1. Study for three hours nonstop?	8	
2. Get to class five minutes early?	9	
3. Get two A+s in one semester?	6	
4. Study with a study group?	5	
5. Do your homework two days ahead of time?	3	
6. Ask a question in class?	5	
7. Answer a question in class?	2	
8. Get the highest grade in class?	7	
9. Give a Teacher's Day present?	10	
10. Explain something to a classmate?	4	
TOTAL POINTS (Good students will have many points.)	59	

HOW OFTEN DO YOU ...?

	Ex	ME
11. Get to class late?	9	
12. Play hooky (skip class)?	4	
13. Get the lowest grade in class?	2	
14. Fall asleep in class?	9	
15. Fall asleep while the professor is talking?	3	
16. Check your cell phone in class?	10	
17. Lie about why you were absent?	5	
18. Daydream in class?	10	
19. Pretend you understand, but really don't?	10	
20. Lie about why your homework is not done?	7	
TOTAL POINTS (Bad students will have many points.)	69	

↑ Ouch.

What about you?

Really? Wow!	*Get outta town.*	*Me too.*
You're kidding.	*In your dreams.*	*Same here.*
No way!	*Yeah, and I'm Brad Pitt.*	*Ditto.*
Yeah, right!	*You're pulling my leg.*	*I'm the same way.*

10 — All the time / Always / *Every day* / *Almost every day*

9 — As often as possible / Every chance I get / *Every other day* / *Four times a week*

8 — Frequently / Often / *Three times a week* / *Twice a week*

7 — Usually / Generally / *Once a week* / *Four times a month*

6 — Sometimes / Occasionally / *Twice a month* / *Once every two weeks*

5 — Every now and then / On special occasions / *Every month* / *Every other month*

4 — Not too often / Seldom / *Once every three months* / *Four times a year*

3 — Rarely / Very seldom / *Once every four months* / *Three times a year*

2 — Hardly ever / Once in a blue moon / *Twice a year* / *Once a year*

1 — Never ever / When hell freezes over / *Not on your life* / *When pigs fly*

4 SHOPPING

 22

VOCABULARY VITAMINS

accessories	장신구	instant gratification	사고싶은 것을 즉시 사야하는
all the bells and whistles	부수적인 내용물; 덤	knock-off	유명브랜드의 가짜 상품
baggy	너무 헐렁한	look all over town	온동네를 다 뒤져보다
bargain	매매; 싼 물건	luxurious	고급스러운; 화려한
bargain shopper	할인가격 물건만 사는 사람	mom-and-pop store	구멍가게
big / small selection	종류가 많은 / 종류가 적은	novelty shop	신기한 물건 파는 곳
brand name	상표; 브랜드	one-stop shopping	모든 물품을 갖춘 가게
brand-new	새로운; 갓 출시된	perfume / cologne	향수(여자용) / 콜론(남자용향수)
browse, browsing	둘러보다	plastic (credit cards)	신용카드
cashier	돈 받는 사람	receipt	영수증
champagne taste	고급 취향	refund	환불
cheap (person)	구두쇠; 짠돌이	rip off, ripped off	바가지를 씌우다
cheap merchandise	싼 물건	shop till you drop	쇼핑광
cheap price	싼 가격	shopaholic	쇼핑을 좋아하는; 쇼핑 중독
convenience store	편의점	shopping spree	물건을 많이 사들이다
customer service	고객지원	souvenir shop	기념품 가게
defective	불량품, 결점이 있는	splurge	돈을 펑펑 쓰다
designer label	유명브랜드	street vendor	노점상
dressing room	분장실, 탈의실	tacky	싸구려처럼 보이는
expensive	비싼	the old bait and switch	호객을 위한 속임수 광고
fancy	고급스러운; 고성능의	tightwad	구두쇠
floor model	진열된 상품; 진열품	top-end	가장 좋은 비싼
frugal; thrifty	검소한; 알뜰한	used	중고품; 헌 것
generic	일반브랜드	variety, various, vary	다양한
gyp, gypped	가격은 비싸지만 질이 낮은	wardrobe	소유하고 있는 의복
haggle	흥정하다	warranty; guarantee	교환보장
impulse buyer, shopper	충동구매자	window shopping	구입하지는 않고 구경만 하는 쇼핑

CONVERSATION STARTERS

*This is not an interview. Each question is designed to start a conversation.
Write what you will say, and talk about what you wrote.*

1. **Do you prefer shopping in stores or online?** *What items do you buy online? Why?*
   Half and half. For clothes I go shopping; for books and tech stuff I shop online.

2. **Where do you like to go shopping?** *How often do you go shopping? Who do you go with?*
   I usually go to either Myeong-dong or Apgujeong-dong. They have more variety.

3. **What is the most money you ever spent while shopping?** *Were you sober? (Joke.)*
   Once, I spent 200,000 won on a thick winter jacket in the Lotte Department Store.

4. **If you were given a thousand dollars (1,000,000 won), what would you buy?**
   Hmm. I would get a new iPad and a bunch of new clothes for college. I want to look sharp.

5. **Do you have a favorite brand of clothes?** *Have you ever bought a fake by mistake?*
   Yes. I really like Reebok and Calvin Klein. Once I bought some Channel perfume instead of Chanel.

6. **Do you like to haggle with the sellers?** *Do you ever win? Tell me about it.*
   No, I am too shy. But my older sister does it all the time.

7. **Have you ever taken something back because it was defective?**
   Yes. Once, I took some pants back because the zipper was broken.

8. **Are you an impulse buyer?** *Are you a bargain shopper?*
   No, but my older sister once bought a hat that was too ugly to wear. She tried to give it to me.

---

*Really?   You're kidding.   No way.   Me too!   Say what?   Bummer.
Where?   When?   Why?   Who?   What time?   How?   How long?   How often?
Kind of.   Sometimes.   Half and half.   It depends.*

What about you?

CONVERSATION STARTERS

9. **How many tech devices do you have?** *Which is your favorite? How much did it cost?*
   My father is very high-tech, so he gets me whatever I need. I have an iPhone, iPad, and 27-inch iMac.

10. **How many credit cards do you have?** *What is the last thing you bought with one?*
    I have one credit card. Last weekend I used it to buy some dress shoes.

11. **Where did you get your cell phone?** *What kind is it? Are you satisfied with it?*
    I bought it at Techno Mart last month. It was on sale. I text and take a lot of photos with it.

12. **What is your favorite perfume?** *Makeup? Designer? Cologne?*
    My girlfriend likes Chanel, but I think the best smell is no smell.

13. **Do you shop around to compare prices, or do you buy the first thing you find?**
    I usually buy something right away if I like it. The prices don't vary that much.

14. **Do you ever shop on the Internet?** *What kind of phone do you have? How old is it?*
    Oh yes, I'm addicted. I love to shop online. I rarely go shopping anymore. I hate crowds.

15. **Would you rather have a new phone or new computer?**
    Both! Well, I'd take a new phone so I could record all my class lectures and listen later.

16. **Do you buy a lot of things when you go on vacation?** *What is your favorite souvenir?*
    I try to, but sometimes it doesn't all fit in my luggage when it's time to go home.

Write your own question: _____

Really?   You're kidding.   No way.   Me too!   Say what?   Bummer.
Where?   When?   Why?   Who?   What time?   How?   How long?   How often?
Kind of.   Sometimes.   Half and half.   It depends.

What about you?

MODEL CONVERSATION

At home, listen and repeat five times. Your pronunciation will DEFINITELY improve.

Brad   Hey, Britney, where are you going?

Britney   Shopping. It's a dirty job, but somebody's got to do it.

Brad   Yeah, right. Is Little Miss Cheap actually going to spend some money, or will you just spend the whole afternoon browsing again?

Britney   I'm not <u>cheap</u>, just <u>frugal</u>. I'm not an <u>impulse shopper</u> like you. Remember that girl's T-shirt you bought? Did you ever wear that?

Brad   Hey! The clerk said it was a unisex shirt. Next topic. Who's paying for your shopping spree?

Britney   My father gave me his credit card and told me to get some new clothes for this semester.

Brad   Wow. You hit the jackpot. Where are you going?

Britney   Myeong-dong.

Brad   What will you get?

Britney   Clothes, shoes, cosmetics, perfume, purses. Whatever's on sale.

Brad   It's your birthday. <u>Splurge</u>. Buy something you like, even if it's not on sale. You <u>haggle</u> too much.

Britney   Haggling, that's my hobby.

Brad   Give me a break. You're just cheap. Can I come along and watch you in action?

Britney   OK, but help me this time! Last time all you did was flirt with the salesgirls.

Brad   Say what? I was turning on the charm so they would give you a better price.

Britney   If you say so.

Brad   Are you going to go back to the Lancôme store? I think that pretty salesgirl likes me. She kept winking at me.

Britney   Brad! Get a life. A, she had trouble with her contacts. B, she's a salesgirl. It's her job to be nice!

Brad   Aha. That explains why the phone number she gave me was out of service.

TOP 4 CULTURAL DIFFERENCES

These cultural differences can also be conversation starters. You can ask:
What do you think about number 1? How do you feel about number 2? Which way do you prefer?

1. American shoppers pay sales tax—usually four to eight percent—which is added to the cost of the merchandise. Each town and state sets how much the tax will be, so the tax amount changes from town to town and state to state. Also, the tax amount is not shown until you pay.

2. Most American stores are big—some really big—with few salespeople. Korea has many small shops, and the big stores have many, many salespeople.

3. In Korea, if you handle the merchandise and ask questions, you are expected to buy it. In America, you are not.

4. If an American store is out of a product, and they only have the display model (floor model) left, they will usually offer to sell that to you at a reduced price. The price is lower, but the warranty is just as long.

CULTURE QUESTIONS
Have you ever had a job in sales?
Could you be a good salesperson? Can you face rejection?
Have you ever gone shopping in a foreign country?

VOCABULARY DEVELOPMENT

ACROSS

1. That's _____. Does your father own a bank?
4. No thanks, I'm just _____.
7. My grandfather is a _____. He only believes in saving money, not in spending it.
8. Today is payday. Let's go shop till we _____.
10. My mother is a _____ shopper. She shops only when there is a sale.
11. My mother loves to _____. She'll negotiate till the seller gives up.
12. This material is too _____. There's no way I can afford it.

DOWN

2. My sister is a _____. Shopping is her hobby.
3. I like these _____ pants. They're loose and comfortable.
5. I'm an _____ buyer. I have many shopping regrets.
6. You paid $50? You got _____. I got it for $20.
9. I wouldn't call my mom cheap, but she is _____.
10. Don't buy that cheap stuff. Get a _____ name.

LONGER & SMOOTHER SPEAKING

WRITE ABOUT SHOPPING AND YOUR WARDROBE
Use as many Vocabulary Vitamins as possible.

Write what you will say, and talk about what you wrote.

I'm not into clothes that much. That's why I liked the school uniforms in high school. I had no clothing decisions to make every morning; I just put on my uniform. Luckily, right after I got accepted to this university, my dad gave me his credit card and told me to go get a college <u>wardrobe</u>. I bought mainly jeans and T-shirts, along with a few dresses and skirts for special occasions. I also like <u>baggy</u> clothes. Tight-fitting clothes make me feel fat, so I always buy things loose. I bought some Nike sportswear in Dongdaemun, but they fell apart after the first washing, so now I think they were <u>knock-offs</u>.

My mother is a <u>bargain shopper</u>. She'll shop only when there is a sale. She's frugal when it comes to clothes, but she'll buy top-quality food and electronics. And she buys <u>top-end</u> cosmetics. My father is a <u>big spender</u> on everything except food. He says it all tastes the same to him. It's a good thing Mom buys his clothes for him because he has goofy tastes in clothes. Once, he bought this green checkered suit. My mom screamed, "What were you thinking?" That was an <u>impulse buy</u>. Dad lied about where he bought it. He said it was at Lotte, but Mom saw a local street vendor with the exact same suits. That was a quiet night at the dinner table.

You could type it on a computer and tape it above. This would check your spelling and grammar! Cool.

CONVERSATION

You are going to have a conversation test, so practice having a shopping conversation.
The more follow-up questions you ask, the higher your grade.
The more vocabulary you use, the higher your grade.
Say what? Yes, make comments, too!

1	Has the same favorite sports brand	6	Has the same favorite color
2	Likes to shop in Myeong-dong	7	Likes baggy clothes
3	Goes shopping twice a month	8	Likes dressy clothes
4	Hates to go shopping	9	Gets lost when shopping
5	Has more than five pairs of shoes	10	Got ripped off while shopping

1. Have you ever gotten ripped off while shopping?
2. Do you buy books online or in stores?
3. Do you ever get lost when shopping?
4. Do you have a lot of jewelry?
5. Do you have a single- or double-breasted suit?
6. Do you have any really high heels?
7. Do you like to go shopping? Why not?
8. Do you like to shop online?
9. Do you like your clothes baggy or tight?
10. Do you prefer to casual or dressy clothes?

Really?   No kidding.   No way!   Say what?   Me too!   Bummer.

What about you?

STATION

THE MORE MISTAKES YOU MAKE, THE BETTER!
If you are not making any mistakes, you are probably
(1) saying nothing, or (2) saying something you memorized.
This is a conversation class, not a grammar class.
Look at the book cover again. What does it say? **No rules, just talking, long and loud.**

11	Has a double-breasted suit	16	Has the same favorite perfume
12	Has lots of jewelry	17	Buys books online
13	Has heels higher than 4 inches (10 cm)	18	Shops only when there are sales
14	Prefers to shop online	19	Has had a job in a clothing store
15	Has returned defective merchandise	20	Still uses cash to shop

11. Do you use cash or a card when you shop?
12. Do you wait until there are sales?
13. How many pairs of shoes do you have?
14. Have you ever worked in a clothing store?
15. Have you ever returned defective merchandise?

16. How often do you go shopping?
17. What is your favorite color in clothes?
18. What is your favorite perfume?
19. What is your favorite sports brand?
20. Where do you like to shop?

Where?   When?   Why?   Who?   How?   What time?   How often?

What about you?

5 MOVIES

Scan and find the tracks.

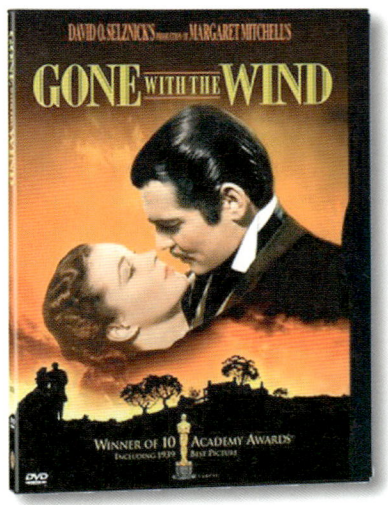
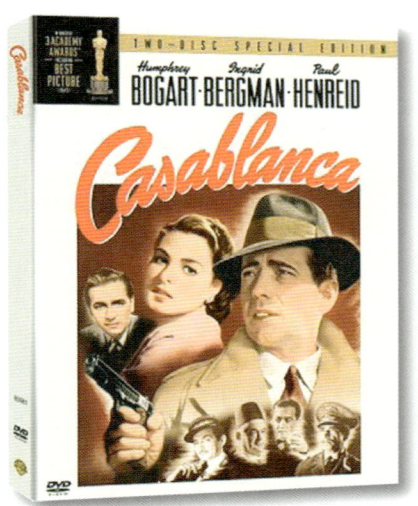

If you have not seen these movies, you cannot understand American culture.

 27

VOCABULARY VITAMINS

animation	만화영화
based on	~에 기초한, 근거한
character actor	성격파 배우
chemistry	두 사람 간의 끌리는 에너지
chick flick / date flick	여성용 영화 / 남녀 모두 좋아하는 영화
cut to the chase	주요장면으로 바로 넘어가다
director / producer	감독 / 프로듀서
ensemble cast	주역없이 여러 유명배우들이 출연함
far-fetched	믿을 수 없는
femme fatale	요부, 팜므파탈
flashback	회상을 하며 장면을 바꿔 넣는 것
genre	장르
girl-next-door type	보통의, 평범한 소녀
gory	지나치게 피를 많이 흘리는
happy ending	행복한 결말
hard to follow	난해한, 이해하기 어려운
leading man / lady	남자 / 여자 주인공
macho; tough guy	왕초, 터프가이
parody	풍자적인 개작
platonic relationship	정신적인, 관념적인 관계
plot twist	반전
plot / theme	구성 / 주제
predictable	너무 뻔한 (예상가능한)
remake	재 영화한 작품
sappy	너무 감상적인
sequel	속편
slow	너무 느린 전개의
snooty rich type	상류층의 거만한, 오만한
sold out	매진
special effects	특수효과
supporting actor	조연배우
surprise ending	(영화 등) 예상치 못한 결말
the bad guy; villain	악당

BASIC MOVE TYPES & PLOTS

amnesia	기억 상실
black comedy	블랙코미디
boy meets girl, boy loses girl, boy gets girl	
buddy film	두 배우가 콤비를 이룬 영화
Cinderella story	신데렐라
coming-of-age film	성장영화
dialog-driven movie	대화가 주요된
film noir	느와르 영화, 필름 느와르
historical drama	사극영화
horror movie	공포영화
love triangle	삼각관계
musical	음악의, 뮤지컬
prison film	감옥영화
puppy love	어린 나이의 사랑, 풋사랑
revenge	복수
road film	로드 무비
science fiction	SF, 공상과학영화
slapstick comedy	슬랩스틱 코메디
slasher film	공포영화
tearjerker	눈물나게 하는 영화
unrequited love	짝사랑
Western; cowboy movie	카우보이 영화

 28 **CONVERSATION STARTERS**

This is not an interview. Each question is designed to start a conversation.

1. **What is your favorite Korean movie?** *How many times have you seen it?*
   My favorite is Thieves. *It has both Jeon Ji-yeon and Kim Hye-soo in it.*

   _____

2. **What is your favorite English-language movie?** *When does it take place?*
   My favorite is The Pianist *with Adrien Brody. It takes place during World War II.*

   _____

3. **Where does your favorite movie take place?** *What time span does it cover?*
   It takes place in Europe, Poland mainly. It covers about five years, from the start to the end of the war.

   _____

4. **What is your favorite movie genre?** *What kind of movies do your parents like?*
   I like action-adventure superhero movies, like The Avengers *and the* Iron Man *series.*

   _____

5. **Which movie have you seen the most?** *What is the last movie you went to?*
   I've seen Thieves *about ten times. The last movie I went to at the theater was the new* Avengers *movie.*

   _____

6. **How often do you watch movies?** *English-language movies? No subtitles?*
   I go to the movies once a month, and once a week I download one. I need the subtitles.

   _____

7. **What is the funniest movie that you have ever seen?** *The worst movie?*
   Let's see. Probably Dumb and Dumber. *The worst movie was any drama with Jim Carrey.*

   _____

8. **Where is your favorite place to see a movie?** *How often do you go there? Cost?*
   I love going to the movies at Techno Mart. The sound system is great. I go about once a month.

   _____

> Really?   You're kidding.   No way.   Me too!   With subtitles?
> Where?   When?   Why?   Who?   What time?   How?   How long?   How often?
> Kind of.   Sometimes.   Half and half.   It depends.

What about you?

CONVERSATION STARTERS  29

9. **Who are your favorite male and female Korean movie stars?**
   I love Won Bin and Jang Dong-gun. Females I like are Jeon Ji-hyun and Shim Min-ah.

10. **Who are your favorite male and female American movie stars?** *Chinese? Japanese?*
    I like Brad Pitt and that guy in Thor, *Chris Hemsworth. I really like Scarlett Johansson and Qi Shu.*

11. **Have you ever fallen asleep in a movie theater?** *What movie were you seeing?*
    Yeah, twice. During Man of Steel, *that Superman movie, and* Meet Joe Black *with Brad Pitt.*

12. **Do you like animated movies?** *Musicals? Scary movies? Romantic comedies?*
    Oh, yes. My favorite is Frozen. *The color was fantastic. The story gave me chills.* (Get it? *Frozen,* chills?)

13. **Have you ever seen a movie or TV star in person?** *How did it happen?*
    Yeah, once I saw Kim Hye-soo. She was filming a commercial in my neighborhood.

14. **What is your favorite TV show?** *Who are the stars? Do you watch any American TV?*
    I like Superstar K *because the music's great. The stars are different every year.*

15. **What is the worst movie you've ever seen?** *Do you like scary movies? Gory movies?*
    No way. I hate scary movies. I hate horror movies and slasher movies.

16. **Who do you like best?** *Superman? Batman? Spider-Man? Avengers? Captain America?*
    I like Batman. His life story is more interesting. The other movies are all just special effects.

Write your own question: _____

> Really? You're kidding. No way. Me too! With subtitles?
> Where? When? Why? Who? What time? How? How long? How often?
> Kind of. Sometimes. Half and half. It depends.

What about you?

MODEL CONVERSATION

At home, listen and repeat five times. Your pronunciation will DEFINITELY improve.

Brad	Hey Britney, how was your weekend?
Britney	Great. I went to the movies and saw The Avengers 12.
Brad	You're kidding, right? The Avengers already has eleven <u>sequels</u>? Amazing. How was it?
Britney	Actually, kind of <u>predictable</u>. Blah blah blah, <u>special effects</u>, climactic fight, the good guys win.
Brad	So, why did you like it?
Britney	Well, the characters are evolving, and there is better <u>chemistry</u> between the <u>ensemble cast</u>. And there was a great <u>plot twist</u>.
Brad	Well, what was the twist?
Britney	I don't want to spoil it for you. Have you seen any good movies lately?
Brad	I saw Talk To Me Slowly. It was a <u>dialog-driven</u> movie and I fell asleep. I wasted my money.
Britney	Bummer. Do you remember the plot?
Brad	No, but I remember they talked really slowly. Live and learn. Oh, a few weeks ago I saw the new animated movie by Disney. Now that was an awesome movie.
Britney	Wow. Why did you like it so much?
Brad	It was so realistic. The villain was actually an English professor who did not give any A-pluses. Oh, I could so relate!
Britney	Really? Wait. You're kidding, right?
Brad	Yeah, but I had you going.
Britney	Fine. Just for that I'll tell you the <u>plot twist</u> in The Avengers. There's a new superhero called Confusion Man. He makes people confused.
Brad	Wait, Confucian Man? He makes people calm?
Britney	Confused. He's Confusion Man, not Confucian Man.
Brad	Oh. Yeah, I see. I think. I'm already confused.

MY TOP KOREAN MOVIE
Korean male & female movie star
Korean male & female TV star
Favorite American movie
American male & female star
My favorite recent movie
My top three movies of all time

TOP 5 CULTURAL DIFFERENCES

These cultural differences can also be conversation starters. You can ask:
What do you think about number 1? How do you feel about number 2? Which way do you prefer?

1. Americans mainly see only American or English-language movies. Koreans see movies from all over the world.

2. In Korea, some movies may be censored for sexual content. American movies have no such censorship. The US and Korea both give movies different ratings based on how much sex, violence, and profanity they contain.

3. Big American movie stars do not often make commercials or appear in ads in America. However, you will see stars such as Leonardo DiCaprio in advertisements in Asia and Europe.

4. American movie stars used to rarely appear on TV shows. However, big stars are starting to appear in many big-budget cable TV shows.

5. Some TV stars in American make fabulous amounts of money, but they still want to succeed in movies, which are the "big time" for actors and actresses.

CULTURE QUESTIONS
Is it OK for paparazzi to invade people's privacy?
Do movie stars have too much plastic surgery?
Should Korean movie and sports stars get special treatment during their military service?

RANK (1-10) YOUR FAVORITE KINDS OF MOVIES
Action-adventure
Animation
Comedy
Drama
Slasher, Horror
Musical
Romantic Comedy
Romantic Drama
Science Fiction
Thriller

VOCABULARY DEVELOPMENT

ACROSS
1. Too much crying. I don't like _____ movies.
4. The romantic leads had good _____.
6. He looks violent and plays a mean _____.
8. It started with a _____ to his childhood.
10. There were seven big stars in that _____ cast.
12. What is your favorite movie _____?
13. He usually plays the _____ rich type.

DOWN
2. That plot was too _____. No suspense.
3. Too much blood! I don't like _____ movies.
5. I don't like _____-driven movies. There's way too much talking.
7. What kind of person watches _____ movies? Who likes watching bloody, gory death?
9. She's sexy and usually plays the _____ *fatale*.
11. Wow! His enemy turned out to be his sister, whom he'd never met. Now that is a _____ twist!

LONGER & SMOOTHER SPEAKING

WRITE ABOUT YOUR FAVORITE MOVIE, or favorite kind of movie.
Use as many Vocabulary Vitamins as possible.

Write what you will say, and talk about what you wrote.

I'm a big movie fan. My favorite movies are the big-budget superhero movies, like Spider-Man, Batman, Iron Man, and especially the Avengers series. In The Avengers I like their <u>ensemble cast</u>, and in Iron Man I like the <u>chemistry</u> between Iron Man and his secretary. I must say that all the plots are kind of <u>predictable</u>: "All starts out good, the world gets into great danger, the heroes save the world." Not much suspense there. Now that I think about it, all the movies kind of blend together in my memory, so it's hard right now to tell them apart—what exactly happened in which movie. All those movies are made according to the same formula, I think, to make them good <u>date movies</u>. They have <u>macho</u> guys, big action scenes, <u>femme fatales</u>, snappy dialog, and evil villains.

I love all kinds of movies, except for <u>horror</u> movies and especially <u>slasher</u> movies. I just don't get why they make those movies and why people watch them. I also don't get movies about time-travel; I just get confused and fall asleep. And I saw Inception twice and I still don't get it. Well, once I dreamed I got it, but then I woke up and lost it.

You could type it on a computer and tape it above. This would check your spelling and grammar! Cool.

Conversation Station

But first, MOVIE TRIVIA CONTEST! Get extra points if you're the first group that names 5:

Movies with sequels	Animated movies	Superhero movies	Musical movies
Science fiction	Tom Cruise movies	Horror movies	Historical dramas
Take place in Europe	Leonardo DiCaprio	A number in the title	A city in the title

Do you prefer ...?
1. Korean movies or English movies?
2. Chinese or Japanese movies?
3. Musicals or animated movies?
4. Girl groups or boy bands?

Who / What is your favorite ...?
1. Classic movie? Movie this year?
2. Korean movie star? American?
3. Korean singing star? American?
4. Korean TV show? Comedian?

How often do you ...?
1. See an English movie?
2. Download music? Legally?
3. Play a computer game for 4 hours?
4. Watch movies until 4 a.m.?

Have you ever ...?
1. Seen a movie or TV star in person?
2. Seen a famous singer in person?
3. Seen them film at a TV studio?
4. Seen them film at a movie location?

When was the last time you ...?
1. Went to the movies?
2. Fell asleep in a movie? In class?
3. Saw an English movie?
4. Legally downloaded a movie?

Do you ...?
1. Cry at movies? Cry after a test? (joke)
2. Download movies illegally?
3. Sneak food into movies?
4. Get to movies late? Sneak in food?

LIKE to DISLIKE
I love, I enjoy, It's OK, so-so, I don't care for, I dislike, I hate, I can't stand

FREQUENCY
pretty often, hardly ever, never, 200 times a day, once a week, twice a month, 4 times a year

HOW LONG AGO?
last night, yesterday, 2 days ago, last week, 2 weeks ago, 4 months ago, I can't remember

Really?   You're kidding.   No kidding.   No way.   Say what?   Bummer.   Me too.
Where?   When?   Why?   Who?   What time?   How?   How long?   How often?
Kind of.   Sort of.   Sometimes.   Half and half.   It depends.

What about you?

Guess That Movie!

YOU HAVE 15 QUESTIONS.
Your partner will think of a popular movie that you should have seen or know about.
You will try to guess the movie. Use the questions below. DO NOT SKIP any questions.
Then it's your turn. You think of a movie. Give minimal information to make them ask many questions.

QUESTIONS

1. What kind of movie is it?
2. Where does it take place?
3. When does it take place?
4. How long a time span does it cover?
5. It is an old classic or a modern movie?
6. Does it have a sequel? / Is it a sequel?
7. Is it a true story?
8. Does it have an ensemble cast?
9. Did it win any Academy Awards?
10. How old are the stars?
11. Describe the leading man and leading lady.
12. What is the basic plot?
13. Are there any major plot twists?
14. Does the title have a number or city or place in it?
15. How many words are in the title? What is the first letter of the title?

EXAMPLE ANSWERS

It's a science fiction / comedy / buddy film.
It takes place in Europe / Japan / Rome.
It takes place in the recent past / during World War II.
It covers about five years / a week / a month.

EXAMPLE DESCRIPTIONS

The Wolf of Wall Street is a comedy based on a true story. It takes place in New York about ten years ago. The time span is about four years.

Schindler's List is a historical drama based on a true story. It takes place in Europe during World War II, and the time span is about five years.

Basic movie types	Is it a(n) …?	Basic Plots
action-adventure	murder mystery	boy meets girl, boy loses girl, boy gets girl
animation	musical	amnesia (can't remember)
black comedy	romantic comedy	buddy film
comedy / slapstick comedy	romantic drama	coming-of-age film
crime	science fiction	mistaken identity
drama	slasher film	prison film
film noir	tearjerker	puppy love
historical drama	thriller	road film
horror movie	war movie	unrequited love
melodrama	Western / cowboy movie	love triangle

6 FOOD & RESTAURANTS

Scan and find the tracks.

Say, these students could use a matchmaker.

 32

VOCABULARY VITAMINS

all-you-can-eat buffet	원하는 만큼 먹을 수 있는 부페
atmosphere	(식당 등의) 분위기
brown bag lunch	도시락(갈색 종이 봉투)
brunch	아침겸 점심
chocoholic	초콜릿 중독
complimentary	무료의
delicious	맛있는
diet	식품, 체중 조절을 위한 식사
drive-through	차에서 음식을 주문할 수 있는
eat in or take out?	여기서 드시나요, 가지고 가시나요?
ethnic food	민속음식
fancy food	비싼 음식
fast food	McDonald's, KFC
food poisoning	식중독
foodie, gourmet	식도락가, 미식가
free refills	리필(무료로 채워주는)
freebie	무료의, 경품의
high- / low-calorie	열량이 높은 / 열량이 낮은
high- / low-cholesterol	높은 / 낮은 콜레스테롤
junk food	candy, pastry, chocolate
leftovers	남은 음식, 찌꺼기
messy eater	음식을 흘리면서 먹는 사람
mouth-watering	군침이 돌게 하는
my treat; it's on me	내가 지불할게
nibble	조금씩 계속 먹다
nutritious	영양있는
pick up the tab	음식값을 지불하다
picky eater	편식하는
pig out	돼지처럼 많이 먹다
ritzy; fancy restaurant	고급 식당
salt / pepper	소금 / 후추
sip / guzzle	조금씩 마시다 / 벌컥벌컥 마시다
stuffed	아주 배부르게 먹은
sweet tooth	달콤한 음식 (초콜릿, 초콜릿 사탕)
theme restaurant	주제가 있는 실내장식의 식당
throw up (NOT "overeat")	구토하다
upset stomach	배탈
vegetarian	채식주의자

RESTAURANT FOOD CATEGORIES	
appetizer	입맛 돋우는 음식, 전채요리
dessert	후식
main dish	주요리
side dish	반찬 (주요리 외의 요리)

RESTAURANT PEOPLE	
chef: the Hilton / cook: Burger King	
hostess	(음식점의) 호스티스
waiter / waitress	웨이터 / 웨이트리스

TASTE	
hot	뜨거운 = temperature 온도
spicy	양념이 많이 된, 매운 = taste
bland	맛이 담백한 (not spicy)
fresh / stale	신선한 / 신선도가 떨어진
sweet / sour	단맛 / 신맛

STEAK	
raw	날것의, 익히지 않은
rare	살짝 익힌
medium	중간정도로 익힌
well-done	완전히 익힌
burnt	(음식이) 탄

PIZZA	
thin / thick crust	얇은 / 두꺼운 피자
deep-dish / pan pizza	매우 두꺼운 / 얇은 피자

CHICKEN	
white meat / dark meat	가슴살 / 닭다리
crispy / greasy	바삭한 / 기름기 있는
fried / grilled / baked	튀긴 / 구운 / 오븐에 구운

CHIPS: potato chips, Doritos, nachos, Pringles
DIPS: bean, jalapeno, guacamole, salsa

CONVERSATION STARTERS

Remember, conversation is KING.

1. **What is your favorite Korean food?** *Your favorite Western food?*
   My favorite Korean food is kimchi jjigae. And my favorite Western food is pizza.

2. **How often do you eat out?** *How often do you get food delivered? How often do you pay?*
   I eat out every day on my way home from school, usually kimbap.

3. **Do you like buffet restaurants?** *Do you pig out? How many times do you go back?*
   Yes, I love buffets. When I go to all-you-can-eat places, I eat till I am stuffed.

4. **Do you have a sweet tooth?** *Do you like desserts?*
   I have a sweet tooth. I love dessert and chocolate. I'm a chocoholic.

5. **Are you picky about your food?** *Are you a picky eater?*
   No, I eat anything. I'm hungry all the time. Well, I don't eat food that is moving.

6. **Do you cook?** *What do you cook the most? The best? How often do you cook?*
   I cook kimchi jjigae about twice a month. It tastes OK. I want to try to make a pizza from scratch.

7. **What percentage of your diet is junk food?** *Have you ever eaten food that made you sick?*
   About 30% because I eat on my way home from school. Once, on vacation, I ate some bad seafood.

8. **What did you have for lunch today? / What are you doing for lunch today?**
   I had bibimbap in the student cafeteria. / I'm meeting my friends off campus.

**Really?   You're kidding.   No kidding.   No way.   Say what?   Bummer.   Me too.
Where?   When?   Why?   Who?   What time?   How?   How long?   How often?
Kind of.   Sort of.   Sometimes.   Half and half.   It depends.**

What about you?

CONVERSATION STARTERS

9. **Do you prefer home cooking or restaurant food?** *Honestly, is your mother a good cook?*
   My mother's a great cook, so I prefer home cooking.

10. **What's your favorite kind of pizza?** *When was the last time you ate pizza?*
    Any kind, anywhere. But if I had to pick one, I would say Domino's.

11. **What kind of food do you usually have delivered?** *How often?*
    We order Chinese food about twice a month, every other weekend. We all love jajangmyeon.

12. **Do you have a favorite coffee shop or pub in your neighborhood?**
    Not in my neighborhood, but near school there's a coffee shop where I meet my friends.

14. **What is your favorite side dish at a pub?** *Are you a regular anywhere?*
    I like golbaengi, and sometimes dubu kimchi. I'm not a regular anywhere. I like trying new places.

13. **Do you prefer a small amount of fancy food or a lot of regular food?**
    I like a lot of regular food. I hate to leave a restaurant hungry.

15. **Do you usually eat breakfast?** *Where do you eat at school? What time?*
    Rarely. I generally just pick up a snack on my way to school.

16. **Do you like expensive coffee, like at Starbucks?** *How much coffee do you drink per day?*
    Oh, yes, I love good coffee. You could call me a coffee connoisseur. But I hate cold coffee.

Write your own question. _____

> *Really? You're kidding. No kidding. No way. Say what? Bummer. Me too.*
> *Where? When? Why? Who? What time? How? How long? How often?*
> *Kind of. Sort of. Sometimes. Half and half. It depends.*

What about you?

MODEL CONVERSATION

At home, listen and repeat five times. Your pronunciation will DEFINITELY improve.

Brad   Hey, Britney, have you had lunch yet?

Britney   No. I just got out of class, and I'm <u>starving</u>. I have class from 9:00 to 1:00 straight. What about you? Have you eaten yet?

Brad   No. I'm <u>starving</u> too. Do you want to go <u>check out</u> that new Chinese pizza place?

Britney   You're kidding, right?

Brad   No, I hear it's the next big thing.

Britney   Maybe next time. Pizza takes too long. I'm hungry now!

Brad   Got it. What about Mexican food?

Britney   Mexican is OK. What place do you have in mind?

Brad   There's a new Mexican place right near the copy shop. Second floor.

Britney   Naah. I've been there. The portions are small, and the food is too <u>spicy</u>. And it's expensive.

Brad   Well, excuse me. Do you have any place in mind?

Britney   What about that <u>buffet</u> Mexican restaurant? Big portions, low prices.

Brad   No, then I'll <u>pig out</u> and fall asleep in my next class.

Britney   Whoa! This is getting complicated. I'm hungry! Think of something. Chop-chop.

Brad   What about a couple of sandwiches in the coffee shop?

Britney   That'll work. Then I should be perky for my afternoon classes. No nodding off.

Brad   Which coffee shop? Pick one. All coffee tastes the same to me.

Britney   Me too.

Brad   Oh, really? I thought you were a coffee <u>connoisseur</u>.

Britney   That's only when my date is buying.

Rank your favorites 1 to 10
Baskin Robbins
Burger King
Domino's
Dunkin' Donuts
KFC
McDonald's
Pizza Hut
Popeye's
Taco Bell
Krispy Kreme

TOP 7 CULTURAL DIFFERENCES

These cultural differences can also be conversation starters. You can ask:
What do you think about number 1? How do you feel about number 2? Which way do you prefer?

1. Americans never yell to get a waiter's or waitress's attention. It would be considered rude.

2. In America, they take your drink order first. That way, while you are looking over the menu, they are making your drink. (See, they have their drink already.) 👉

3. Americans tip servers and bartenders between 10% and 20% (10 being below average and 20 being above average).

4. Food in American restaurants takes longer to prepare. Therefore, many American restaurants have crackers or bread on the table to keep people from starving while they are waiting.

5. It is good American manners to chew your food with your mouth closed, and not to talk while chewing.

6. Koreans share their food and often eat from a common bowl for dishes such as kimchi jjigae. Americans are worried about germs and do not like to eat out of a common bowl.

7. Americans usually pay their own way (except on dates), so they don't need to say, "Let's go Dutch."

CULTURAL QUESTIONS
Some Korean restaurants started refusing to allow children to enter because of lawsuits involving children who were injured in a restaurant. What do you think?
What do you think of tipping? If you could make a law, would there be tipping or no tipping?

VOCABULARY DEVELOPMENT

ACROSS
1. This food has no taste. It's too _____.
5. Ask the _____ for a table on the patio.
7. I'm starving. Let's order an _____ now and the main dish later.
9. All you eat is candy and _____ food. Eat an apple!
11. That's wine! Don't guzzle it. _____ it.
12. I'm _____. I couldn't eat another bite.
13. Will that be eat in or take _____?

DOWN
2. No more, thank you. I'm leaving room for _____.
3. I like Popeye's _____ fried chicken the best.
4. Mom, please cook! I'm getting tired of _____.
6. Bring some water, please. This food is really _____.
8. They have a great seafood _____. I always eat till I'm stuffed.
10. Oh, my pants are too tight. I need to go on a _____.

LONGER & SMOOTHER SPEAKING

This will help you speak longer and more smoothly. Try to use some Vocabulary Vitamins. Write what you will say, and talk about what you wrote.

WRITE ABOUT FOOD AND RESTAURANTS

I am not a picky eater. I eat anything. I prefer big portions of anything to small portions of fancy food. My favorite Western food is pizza. The thicker, the better. I like the super-supreme, deluxe, combo, the works. The only thing I don't like on my pizza is corn. I like rice dishes more than noodle dishes, such as jajangmyeon. I also like spicy food such as buldak. I like spicy food, but I cannot eat food or drink coffee if the temperature is too hot. To be honest, what I really like is junk food. I love chocolate, donuts, and ice cream. Oh, and I love potato chips and bread.

My second-favorite American food is Popeye's crispy fried chicken. We usually get pizza or fried chicken every other Saturday, so my mom doesn't have to cook. On my birthday, we usually go to TGIF's. I like their festive atmosphere, but they're kind of expensive.

On Fridays after class, I usually meet my friends off campus, and we eat out. We usually have Korean food, either chicken or galbi. I don't like to drink because my face turns red, but I enjoy the mood. I used to have a curfew, but now I can hang out till whenever. When I get home, I always have the midnight munchies, so I hope my mom has some leftovers.

You could type it on a computer and tape it above. This would check your spelling and grammar! Cool.

Conversation Station

But hey, first, what about some current events? *Good idea.*
What did you do last night? Last weekend? Last summer vacation?
What will you do after class? Tonight? This weekend? This winter vacation?

Ask any question, ask any group of questions, or use a die. Conversation is KING.

What is your favorite …?
1. Kind of pizza? Western food?
2. Bennigan's, Outback, or TGIF?
3. Burger King, McDonald's, or VIPS?
4. Ethnic food? Thai? Mexican?
5. Chicken restaurant?

When was the last time you …?
1. Cooked? Cooked for your family?
2. Went to a buffet restaurant?
3. Ate Chinese food? Japanese?
4. Ate a hamburger? Pizza? Chicken?
5. Pigged out? Ate after midnight?

Do you …?
1. Eat at school? Where? When?
2. Eat breakfast every day?
3. Eat out on your birthday?
4. Ever go on a diet?
5. Like thick or thin crust on pizza?

Do you prefer …?
1. Western food or Korean food?
2. Appetizers or dessert?
3. Beef or pork kalbi?
4. KFC or Popeye's?
5. Chinese food or Japanese food?

Are you …?
1. Going to buy me supper tonight?
2. A picky eater? A messy eater?
3. Always hungry? Always thirsty?
4. A fast eater? Do you finish first?
5. A regular at a certain beer pub?

How often do you …?
1. Go to TGIF, Bennigan's, or Outback?
2. Do the dishes? Clean your room?
3. Drink coffee? Drink alcohol?
4. Eat Western food? Chinese? Pizza?
5. Get food delivered? Chicken?

Really?   You're kidding.   No way.   Bummer.   Say what?   Me too!
Where?   When?   Why?   Who?   What time?   How?   How long?   How often?
Kind of.   Sort of.   Sometimes.   Half and half.   It depends.

FOOD & FITNESS FREQUENCY

HOMEWORK: Fill in the blanks with your answers. For example, look at question 1. If you exercise three times a week, give yourself an 8. Fill in all the blanks in the second column and then add them up.

CLASSWORK: Interview two other students. Write down their answers.
When you answer, try to use a phrase in regular type and a phrase in italics.

Brad	*How often do you exercise?*	**Example Conversation**
Britney	*Every now and then. About once a month.*	
Brad	*Really? You look pretty fit.*	
Britney	*What about you? How often do you exercise?*	
Brad	*Frequently. About twice a week.*	
Britney	*No way! You haven't exercised since high school!*	

HOW OFTEN DO YOU ...?

	Ex	ME
1. Pig out?	10	
2. Start a diet?	9	
3. Drink alcohol?	6	
4. Eat dessert?	9	
5. Eat breakfast?	3	
6. Eat after 10 p.m.?	1	
7. Cook for your family?	2	
8. Eat junk food?	7	
9. Go to bed after midnight?	5	
10. Drink coffee?	4	
TOTAL POINTS (Unhealthy students will have many points.)	56	

HOW OFTEN DO YOU ...?

	Ex	ME
1. Exercise?	2	
2. Work out in a gym?	1	
3. Jog for at least thirty minutes?	1	
4. Ride a bicycle?	9	
5. Play a team sport?	3	
6. Go swimming?	5	
7. Go mountain climbing?	5	
8. Do yoga?	1	
9. Sleep till noon?	10	
10. Do aerobics?	2	
TOTAL POINTS (Healthy students will have many points.)	39	

Say what?

What about you?

Really? Wow!	Get outta town.	Me too.
You're kidding.	In your dreams.	Same here.
No way!	Yeah, and I'm Brad Pitt.	Ditto.
Yeah, right!	You're pulling my leg.	I'm the same way.

10 — All the time / Always / *Every day* / *Almost every day*

9 — As often as possible / Every chance I get / *Every other day* / *Four times a week*

8 — Frequently / Often / *Three times a week* / *Twice a week*

7 — Usually / Generally / *Once a week* / *Four times a month*

6 — Sometimes / Occasionally / *Twice a month* / *Once every two weeks*

5 — Every now and then / On special occasions / *Every month* / *Every other month*

4 — Not too often / Seldom / *Once every three months* / *Four times a year*

3 — Rarely / Very seldom / *Once every four months* / *Three times a year*

2 — Hardly ever / Once in a blue moon / *Twice a year* / *Once a year*

1 — Never ever / When hell freezes over / *Not on your life* / *When pigs fly*

7 SPORTS & EXERCISE

 37 **VOCABULARY VITAMINS**

10K race	10킬로미터 경주
marathon	마라톤, 42 km
amateur athlete	아마추어 운동선수
athletic	운동의
athletic scholarship	체육장학금
awkward	서투른
beer belly	술배
calisthenics	준비체조, 미용체조
club membership	클럽회원권
couch potato	움직이기 싫어하는 사람
crash diet	속성 다이어트
endurance	내구력
exhausted	매우 지친
fit	건강한
fitness freak	운동 중독자
flab, flabby	군살이 있는
graceful	우아한
gym	체육관
hard core	철저한 신념이나 흥미를 가진
health club	헬스클럽
in / out of shape	몸매 좋은 / 나쁜
jock / nerd	운동만 잘하는 / 샌님
killer abs	잘 단련된 복근
last one picked	팀에서 제일 못하는 선수
Little League	어린이 운동팀 (야구)
muscular	근육질의
natural athlete	선천적인 운동선수
No pain, no gain.	고진감래
pace	보조, 걷는 속도
pace yourself	페이스를 조절하다
panting	헐떡거리는
PE: physical education	체육
PE uniform	체육복
pooped	지쳐버린
professional athlete	프로선수
sprint	전력질주하다
stretch	스트레치하다
sweat	땀 (흘리다)
track and field	육상 경기
warm up	준비운동
workout, work out	운동
yoga / Pilates	요가 / 필라테스
cheerleader	치어리더
coach	코치
referee; umpire	심판
ache; sore	통증, 쑤시다
blister	물집
muscle cramp	근육경련
pull a muscle	근육을 무리하게 쓰다
sprain	접질리다

SPORTS

aerobics
archery
badminton
baseball
basketball
bowling
boxing
fencing
figure skating
football
golf
gymnastics
hockey
ice skating
jogging
marathon
mountain climbing
ping pong
rollerblading
rugby
skiing
snowboarding
soccer
speed skating
swimming
table tennis
tennis
volleyball

MARTIAL ARTS
hapkido; aikido
judo; jujitsu
karate
kumdo; kendo
MMA
taekwondo
wrestling

Olympics
World Cup
World Series
Super Bowl

 38

CONVERSATION STARTERS

This is not an interview. Each question is designed to start a conversation.

1. **What is your favorite sport or exercise?** *How often do you do it?*
   My favorite sport is tennis, and I play with my brother. We play at least once a week. We're both so-so.

2. **Have you ever won an athletic contest?** *Have you ever participated in a contest?*
   I took taekwondo when I was young, and I won several pumse contests.

3. **What is your favorite sport to watch?** *Do you play on a sports team? Are you any good?*
   I love to watch soccer—any team, any time. My father likes to watch golf.

4. **Can you swim?** *Can you ice skate? Do you ski? Have you ever been injured?*
   Oh, yes, I have been swimming since I was 10. I've skied a few times. I want to try snowboarding.

5. **Is your family athletic?** *Has anyone ever won a contest? Is anyone a world champion?*
   Yes, my whole family plays sports, and my sister is an aerobics instructor.

6. **Do you prefer winter or summer sports?** *Team or individual sports? Indoor, outdoor?*
   I love to ski and swim. I don't like to sweat, so I don't play summer sports.

7. **What is your favorite sports team?** *Who is your favorite sports star?*
   I love the Hyundai Tigers. My favorite basketball team is the LA Lakers.

8. **What is the last sporting event you went to?** *Who did you go with?*
   I went to a soccer game at Jamsil Stadium last month. I went with some friends in my department.

**Really?   You're kidding.   No way.   Bummer.   Say what?   Me too!
Where?   When?   Why?   Who?   What time?   How?   How long?   How often?
Kind of.   Sort of.   Sometimes.   Half and half.   It depends.**

What about you?

CONVERSATION STARTERS

9. **Do you exercise to stay fit or to lose weight?** *Is anyone in your family on a diet?*
   To lose weight. I want to lose about four kilograms. My family is always on a diet.

10. **When was the last time that you played a sport?** *Exercised?*
    I played soccer way back in high school. I scored a goal! Maybe that's why I remember.

11. **Do you belong to a health club?** *Do your parents?*
    Yes, I go three times a week. I use the pool and the treadmill, and I attend a yoga class.

12. **Are you taking any sports at school now?** *What sport did you take in high school?*
    I'm taking jazz dance at school now. In high school I just played soccer every semester.

13. **What is your favorite sport to watch during the Olympics?**
    I like to watch swimming, archery, women's gymnastics, and taekwondo.

14. **Did you ever take taekwondo or kumdo when you were young?**
    I wanted to, but my mom made me take piano. My little brother takes taekwondo.

15. **Have you ever been injured while exercising or playing a sport?**
    Two years ago, I broke my leg while skiing. It wasn't my fault, though—the tree moved.

16. **If you could be an Olympic champion, what sport would it be in?**
    Swimming. I would be famous and have a great body!

Write your own question: _____

> Really?   You're kidding.   No way.   Bummer.   Say what?   Me too!
> Where?   When?   Why?   Who?   What time?   How?   How long?
> Kind of.   Sort of.   Sometimes.   Half and half.   It depends.

What about you?

MODEL CONVERSATION

Brad   Hey, Britney, you're looking great!

Britney   Thanks, Brad. My New Year's resolution was to get <u>in shape</u>.

Brad   Well, you did it. How?

Britney   I took up jogging every morning, and I go to aerobics every other day.

Brad   How far do you jog?

Britney   I run around the park five times—that's about two miles.

Brad   How long does it take?

Britney   About half an hour.

Brad   Did you use any special <u>diet</u>?

Britney   No, I hate to <u>diet</u>. I eat what I want and exercise.

Brad   Well, it's working.

Britney   Are you still working out these days?

Brad   Yeah, I do weight training twice a week.

Britney   How's that going?

Brad   Great. You should see my <u>killer abs</u>. Feel this arm.

Britney   I'll feel your arm, but keep your shirt on. You must really be into <u>working out</u> these days.

Brad   Yeah, but I don't know how long I can keep it up. To get any improvement, I have to work out so hard that I'm <u>sore</u> all the next day.

Britney   Bummer. Well, <u>no pain, no gain</u>.

He's got killer abs.

TOP 5 CULTURAL DIFFERENCES

These cultural differences can also be conversation starters. You can ask:
What do you think about number 1? How do you feel about number 2? Which way do you prefer?

1. The most popular sports in America are professional football, baseball, and basketball. Professional soccer is not very popular.
2. American college sports such as football and basketball are very popular on TV.
3. College sports in America are bigger (more participants, more TV coverage) than in Korea.
4. High school sports in America are bigger than in Korea, mainly because Koreans are very busy preparing for college entrance exams.
5. Koreans (and most Asians) are a group-centered society, while Americans are raised to be individuals. Therefore, school sports in America are used to teach kids teamwork and how to get along in a group.

CULTURE QUESTIONS:
Champion Korean athletes are exempted from military service.
Is this fair? Is this good or bad?
Why is soccer not popular in America?

Team player?

What / Who are your favorite ...
sports to play?
sports to watch?
male athletes?
female athletes?

VOCABULARY DEVELOPMENT

ACROSS
1. At first _____ was painful, but now it's relaxing.
4. I ate too much over the holidays. I'm feeling _____.
5. I played tennis all afternoon and my legs _____.
10. My father is training for the Seoul _____.
11. I played soccer yesterday, but I am so out of _____ that I had to quit after ten minutes.
13. These new jogging shoes do not fit well. I have a big _____ on each foot.

DOWN
2. In this sport, the lowest score wins.
3. You're running too fast. Slow down and _____ yourself.
6. I want to look good on the beach this summer so I'm going on a _____ diet to lose ten pounds.
7. Bad call! That _____ is blind. Or bribed.
8. Kim Yu-na's skating is so _____.
9. Did you ever play Little _____ baseball?
11. I did 50 push-ups in PE and now my arms are _____.
12. You will have to train harder. No _____, no gain.

 41

LONGER & SMOOTHER SPEAKING

WRITE ABOUT YOUR FAVORITE SPORT OR EXERCISE
Use as many Vocabulary Vitamins as possible.

Write what you will say, and talk about what you wrote.

When I was young, my favorite sport was baseball. I played on a Little League team and I was pretty good. I was the pitcher. I played for two years, but then I had to give it up in middle school. These days my favorite sport is soccer, and I play on my department's team. We practice twice a week and play about once a month. I'm pretty good in the first half, but in the second half I am <u>pooped</u>. I need to <u>pace</u> myself better. I'm a pretty good player. I can run faster than most, but my kicking is not so straight. (I think the soccer balls are defective.) Soccer helps me stay <u>in shape</u>. But the beers after the game make me <u>flabby</u>. My goal this year is to get <u>killer abs</u>. That may take dieting and giving up beer. Ah well, <u>no pain, no gain</u>.

I like to watch all kinds of sports on TV: baseball, basketball, volleyball, soccer, tennis, you name it. My favorite teams are the LG Twins and the LA Dodgers. Anyway, I enjoy sports and exercise. I think they are good for both my physical and mental health.

When my father turned 50, he turned into a <u>fitness freak</u>. He goes to the health club every morning before he goes to work, and he plays on the company soccer team. My mom jokes that he's having a mid-life crisis. I think she's joking. Anyway, she also goes to the health club, and they play badminton once a week.

You could type it on a computer and tape it above. This would check your spelling and grammar! Cool.

CONVERSATION

Hey! Ask your professor to give you an extra-points trivia contest!
1. Sit in groups of three. (Hey, sit with your speaking test partners).
2. Your teacher will hand out sheets of paper for you to write on.
3. The first group that can write the answers gets extra points.

1	Has the same favorite sports star	6	Does aerobics
2	Is a couch potato	7	Has taken taekwondo
3	Goes skiing every year	8	Plays tennis
4	Plays on a sports team	9	Is very good at sports
5	Has gone rollerblading	10	Rides a bike

1. Are you a couch potato?
2. Are you good at any sport?
3. Can you ice skate?
4. Can you swim? Dog paddle?
5. Do you belong to a health club?

Questions

6. Do you do aerobics?
7. Do you ever ride a bike?
8. Do you ever work out with weights?
9. Do you like mountain climbing?
10. Do you play on a sports team?

Really? No kidding? No way! Me too! Bummer. Kind of. It depends. Sometimes.

What about you?

STATION

Get extra points if you are the first group to name 5:

Team sports	Winter sports	Year-round sports	Water sports
Individual sports	Summer sports	Sports with a ball	Sports without a ball
Sports Koreans are champions in		Sports you are good at	Sports you are bad at

11	Has never gone skiing	16	Has an athletic family
12	Has the same favorite sport as you	17	Is an excellent swimmer
13	Belongs to a health club	18	Exercises more than twice a week
14	Has not exercised this year	19	Works out with weights
15	Is good at ice skating	20	Goes mountain climbing

11. Do you play tennis?	16. Have you exercised at all this year?
12. Do you ski?	17. How often do you exercise?
13. Have you ever gone rollerblading?	18. Is your family athletic?
14. Have you ever gone skiing?	19. What is your favorite sport?
15. Have you ever taken taekwondo?	20. Who's your favorite sports star?

Questions

Where?   When?   Why?   Who?   What time?   How often?   How many?   How far?

What about you?

8 VACATIONS & TRAVEL

Scan and find the tracks.

 42

VOCABULARY VITAMINS

3-day weekend	주말이 포함된 3일 휴가	peace and quiet	평화롭고 조용한
4 days, 3 nights	3박 4일	peak time / season	바쁜시기
airsick / carsick / seasick	비행기 멀미 / 차멀미 / 멀미	pollution	오염
backpacking	배낭여행	R&R (rest and relaxation)	휴가와 휴양
bags / suitcase / luggage	가방 / 여행가방 / 수하물	relaxing	편안한
bed and breakfast	침실과 조식이 제공되는 민박	reservation	예약
bumper-to-bumper	차가 아주 밀리는	rip off	바가지 씌우다
carry-on	기내 휴대의 수하물	roaming service	휴대전화 로밍 서비스
check in / check out	투숙하여 수속을 밟다	room service	룸서비스
crystal clear	아주 맑은	roughing it	몸으로 고생하는 여행
E.T.A. (estimated time of arrival)	도착 예정 시간	scenic route	경치가 아름다운 도로
folk village	민속마을	scenic view	아름다운 경치
frequent flyer miles	항공 마일리지	semester break	학기 중의 짧은 방학
hassle	싸움, 말다툼(하다)	sightseeing	관광, 구경, 유람
hiking / climbing	하이킹 / 등산	souvenir	기념품
homestay	홈스테이	stressful	긴장이 많은
jet lag	시차병	tentative plans	임시 계획
layover	기착, 경유	tourist trap	가볼만 하나 물가가 비싼 관광지
lost	길을 잃다	travel agency	여행사
non-stop; direct	직행	travel light	최소한의 짐만 갖고 여행하다
one-way / round-trip	편도 / 왕복	trip / vacation	여행 / 방학
overnight trip	1박 여행	turbulence	난기류
package tour	패키지여행	view	경치
pamper, pampered	만족시키다, 만족한	visa	비자
passport	여권	youth hostel	유스호스텔

PLACES TO GO
aquarium
historical district
museum
theme park
zoo

BEACH
jet skiing
parasailing
sailing
scuba diving
snorkeling
sunbathing
surfing
water skiing
windsurfing

SNOW
ski lift
ski pass
snowboarding

MOUNTAINS
camping
white-water rafting

74

 43

CONVERSATION STARTERS

You're going to have a conversation test, so have a real conversation. Use new vocabulary.

1. **Where does your family go on vacation?** *How long does it take to get there?*
   We usually go the east coast. It takes about four hours to drive there.

2. **Have you ever traveled abroad?** *How long did you stay? Who did you go with?*
   Yes, I went to China for a week last year. Getting from the airport to the hotel was a real hassle.

3. **What is your best vacation souvenir?** *Have you ever been ripped off on vacation?*
   I don't have a souvenir, but my father has a big beer mug he brought back from Germany.

4. **What did you do last winter vacation?** *What about last summer? Last weekend?*
   I visited my grandmother in Busan for a month. Last summer I stayed home.

5. **Would you rather go camping or stay at a hotel?** *Have you ever been camping?*
   Oh, I hate bugs. I prefer a nice hotel. I love room service. I stayed at a youth hostel once. Never again.

6. **Do you ever get a part-time job during semester breaks?** *How is the pay?*
   Yes. I usually work at a Chinese restaurant in my neighborhood. The pay is OK, and there's free food.

7. **What was your best vacation ever?** *What about your worst? Your longest?*
   My best vacation was two years ago. My best friend and I went to Europe for a week.

8. **If you could visit anywhere in the world, where would it be?**
   I would love to go to France and see the Louvre Museum. But I hear it's crowded during peak season.

Really?   You're kidding.   No way.   Say what?   Bummer.   Me too.
Where?   When?   Why?   Who?   What time?   How?   How long?   How often?
Kind of.   Sometimes.   Half and half.   It depends.

What about you?

CONVERSATION STARTERS

9. **What is your favorite theme park?** *How often do you go?*
   I really like Caribbean Bay at Everland. It's very crowded but fun.
   _____

10. **Have you ever been in a car accident?** *Have you ever gotten carsick? Airsick? Seasick?*
    Yes, I was in an accident when I was 10. It wasn't bad. I just hit my head, that's all.
    _____

11. **Do you prefer summer or winter vacations?** *Can you swim? Do you ski or snowboard?*
    I prefer summer because I love the beach. I like to swim and scuba dive. I hate being cold.
    _____

12. **Do you travel light?** *Have you ever gotten lost while traveling? Shopping?*
    Yes. No matter where I go or how long I stay, I take only one carry-on bag.
    _____

13. **Have you ever gone on a school trip?** *Did you go to MT this year?*
    I went on a school trip to Japan when I was in middle school. We stayed for a week.
    _____

14. **What is your favorite ski area?** *Where is your favorite beach?*
    My father takes the family to Muju every year, and I like Haeundae beach in Busan.
    _____

15. **Have you ever had jet lag?** *Have you ever had a long layover?*
    I had jet lag when I got back from Europe. Once, I had an eight-hour layover in Hong Kong.
    _____

16. **What will you do this winter / summer vacation?** *What kind? Where? For how long?*
    I'll get my driver's license and go to a computer academy. And of course I'll improve my English.
    _____

Write your own question. _____

> *Really?   You're kidding.   No way.   Say what?   Bummer.   Me too.*
> *Where?   When?   Why?   Who?   What time?   How?   How long?   How often?*
> *Kind of.   Sort of.   Sometimes.   Half and half.   It depends.*

What about you?

MODEL CONVERSATION

Brad   Hey, Britney, what will you do this winter vacation?

Britney   I have <u>tentative plans</u> to go visit my aunt in Canada, but it's not certain yet.

Brad   What's your plan B?

Britney   I'll stay in Korea and maybe get a part-time job. What about you?

Brad   I'm going to Europe with a couple of buddies.

Britney   Lucky you. How long will you be gone?

Brad   Only for two weeks. It was a real <u>hassle</u> getting the airline tickets. We're traveling during <u>peak season</u>.

Britney   I know what you mean. Where will you go?

Brad   Italy. I like the outdoor <u>scenic views</u>, and my friends like the indoors and <u>museums</u>.

Britney   Are you flying <u>direct</u>?

Brad   I wish. We have two <u>layovers</u>, but those were the only tickets we could afford.

Britney   Bummer. Be sure to <u>travel light</u>.

Brad   We will. We're each taking just one <u>carry-on bag</u>. In fact, I'm taking just this school backpack.

Britney   Good luck with that. Will you get <u>roaming service</u> for your phone?

Brad   We all will, in case we get separated.

Britney   I hear that. You get <u>lost</u> in a department store.

Brad   Funny. Ha ha. Have you ever been to Italy?

Britney   Yes. It was awesome. Best vacation ever. I only had one bad experience. We were in a hill town <u>tourist trap</u>. I got <u>ripped off</u> when I bought an autographed picture of Michelangelo.

Brad   Uh, they didn't have cameras in the 1500s.

Britney   Yeah. I know that now!

Do you want some extra points? Bring a vacation photo to class like she did. A+.

My top places to visit in the world
In America
In Seoul
In Korea

TOP 5 CULTURAL DIFFERENCES

These cultural differences can also be conversation starters. You can ask:
What do you think about number 1? How do you feel about number 2? Which way do you prefer?

1. Americans get more vacation days per year, usually at least two weeks, but Korea has more national holidays.
2. Some American businesses close for the whole week between Christmas and New Year's.
3. Americans take their vacations at any time of the year. Vacation days in Korea are usually around the same time of the year (early August).
4. Korean college students are more likely to take vacations together than American students are.
5. Summer break for American schools is much longer than winter break.

CULTURAL QUESTION
Have you had any experience with Chinese, Japanese, American, or Russian tourists in Korea?

Above, roughing it. Below, not.

VOCABULARY DEVELOPMENT

ACROSS
3. That luxurious spa and resort _____ me.
6. We stayed in a _____ hostel. Cheap and OK.
7. We took a _____ tour to Thailand and Vietnam.
8. I hate _____ it. Too much sweat and bugs.
9. I got this _____ of the Eiffel Tower in Paris.
11. That gift shop is a rip-_____. Very expensive.
12. My brother travels _____. He can go for a month with just a backpack.
13. I like traveling, but airports are such a _____.

DOWN
1. We had a four-hour _____ in Seattle.
2. I have _____ plans to go to the beach this weekend, but I may have to work.
4. Where did you go last semester _____?
5. Our hotel room had a great _____ view.
9. I tried snowboarding, but I prefer to _____.
10. We took the scenic _____. It was longer but the views were spectacular.

 46

LONGER & SMOOTHER SPEAKING

WRITE ABOUT YOUR BEST VACATION
Use as many Vocabulary Vitamins as possible.

Write what you will say, and talk about what you wrote.

My favorite vacation of all time was last year. My brother and I went to Seattle for a month to study English. When that was finished, my parents flew in and rented a car, and we drove down the Pacific Coast Highway all the way to San Diego. We flew home from there. During the drive down the coast, my father didn't make any <u>reservations</u>. We would just stop wherever my father chose. The <u>scenic route</u> was awesome. Not every motel was deluxe, and we got <u>ripped off</u> a couple of times, but it was a great adventure. We stayed in a bed and breakfast once, run by some old hippies. That was different. We started out <u>traveling light</u>, but we bought so many souvenirs that we had to buy some more <u>luggage</u> to bring everything home. We studied for a month, and our road trip lasted ten days. Traffic was great until we got near Los Angeles, and then it was <u>bumper-to-bumper</u> all the way to San Diego. Our flight home was great also. My dad arranged it so that we had a one-day <u>layover</u> in Hawaii. Aloha.

You could type it on a computer and tape it above. This would check your spelling and grammar! Cool.

CONVERSATION

By this time, you know all your classmates. Just write the questions below.
Hey! Ask your professor to give you an extra-points trivia contest!

1	Has been to America	6	Has been to China
2	Likes roughing it	7	Likes being pampered
3	Will travel abroad this winter	8	Traveled abroad last summer
4	Has been seasick	9	Went to MT this semester
5	Is a good skier	10	Is a good swimmer

FAVORITES
1. I love — *haggling with the salespeople.*
2. I really like — *hotels with a great view.*
3. I enjoy — *meeting the locals.*
4. so-so — *The food was so-so. I got sick twice.*
5. I don't mind — *the language barrier.*
6. I didn't care for — *the local food.*
7. I don't like — *those pushy vendors.*
8. I hate — *when my luggage is lost.*

PREFERENCES
1. My favorite — *country was France.*
2. My first choice — *is Rome. There's so much to see.*
3. I prefer — *Mexican food.*
4. I like . . . the best — *traveling by train the best.*
5. If I had my choice — *I would have stayed in Paris.*
6. I'd rather not — *go there again. Too polluted.*
7. If I could, I would — *go back to Spain.*
8. My least favorite — *part was the weather.*

1. Are you a good skier?
2. Are you a good swimmer?
3. Have you ever gotten a bad sunburn?
4. Have you ever been ripped off on vacation?
5. Have you ever been to China?
6. Have you ever made a friend on vacation?
7. Did you go to MT this semester?
8. Did you travel abroad last summer?
9. Do you have any great souvenirs?
10. Do you like being pampered?

Really? **No kidding?** **No way!** **Me too!** **Say what?** **Bummer.**

STATION

Sit with your speaking test partners. Get extra points if you're the first group that names 5:

| Island countries | Countries that end in "ia" (India) | South American countries |
| European countries | Muslim countries | US states that begin with M |

11	Has been to Japan	16	Has been to Europe
12	Got ripped off on vacation	17	Made a friend on vacation
13	Will get a job this winter	18	Will go to an academy this winter
14	Travels light	19	Has had a bad sunburn
15	Has a great souvenir	20	Has had jet lag

HOW WAS/WERE THE ...?
1. **Weather** *cold, hot, rainy, sunny, windy, warm, wet, dry*
2. **Hotel** *big, small, cheap, luxurious, swanky*
3. **Hotel room** *big, spacious, too small, clean, great view*
4. **People** *nice, friendly, helpful, unfriendly, rude, crowded*
5. **Transportation** *clean, dirty, convenient, a hassle*
6. **Prices, Shopping** *cheap, expensive, a rip off, knock-offs*
7. **Food** *delicious, expensive, too spicy, too bland*
8. **Sightseeing** *awesome, great, so-so, tourist trap*

QUALITY (from awesome to awful)
Last summer vacation was... The food was...
1. awesome, fantastic, I will always remember
2. superb, excellent, outstanding, wonderful
3. very good
4. so-so, OK, fair
5. bad, not too good, you didn't miss a thing
6. awful, terrible, horrible
7. the pits, it stank, yuck

11. Do you like roughing it?
12. Do you travel light?
13. Have you ever been seasick?
14. Have you ever been to America?
15. Have you ever been to Europe?

16. Have you ever been to Japan?
17. Have you ever had jet lag?
18. Will you go to an academy this winter?
19. Will you travel abroad this winter?
20. Will you work this winter vacation?

Where?   When?   Who?   How?   How long?   How was it?   Would you go again?

9 PRONUNCIATION PRACTICE

Many Korean learners have trouble with these sounds, so here is some practice.
ㅂ, ㅍ = B, P, V, F, PH   ㄹ = L, N, R   ㅈ, ㅊ = CH, J, G, Z   ㅌ = T, TH

You can go to the website *jazzenglish.com* and listen to the pronunciation of these words.

1 FIRST GROUP

	1st	2nd	3rd	4th
1	lack	rack	nack	wack
2	late	rate	wait	Nate
3	lay	ray	way	nay
4	bail	pale	fail	veil
5	bane	pane	feign	vain
6	bill	pill	fill	vill
7	bead	bad	bed	bid
8	beat	bat	bet	bit
9	cheat	chat	Chet	chit
10	meet	mat	met	mitt
11	sheer	cheer	shin	chin
12	lead	read	need	weed
13	led	red	Ned	wed
14	bare	pair	fare	vair
15	base	pace	face	vase
16	Bast	past	fast	vast
17	deed	dad	dead	did
18	eat	at	et	it
19	feast	fast	fest	fist
20	pool	pull	Paul	pole

Pant. That's enough for today.

2

	1st	2nd	3rd	4th
21	feed	fad	fed	fid
22	feet	fat	fet	fit
23	leel	real	kneel	wheel
24	leer	near	rear	we're
25	least	last	lest	list
26	bat	pat	fat	vat
27	bowl	foal	pole	vole
28	beel	peel	feel	veal
29	bye	pie	fie	vie
30	soon	sun	sawn	sewn
31	gin	chin	zen	shin
32	Jane	chain	Zane	Shane
33	gyp	chip	zip	ship
34	life	rife	knife	wife
35	light	right	night	white
36	doon	done	Don	dawn
37	beer	peer	fear	veer
38	berry	Perry	ferry	very
39	ban	pan	fan	van
40	bent	pent	fent	vent

3 SECOND GROUP

	1st	2nd	3rd	4th
41	sheep	cheap	ship	chip
42	he'd	had	head	hid
43	heat	hat	het	hit
44	lip	rip	nip	whip
45	lock	rock	knock	wok
46	low	row	no	woe
47	neat	Nat	net	knit
48	peat	pat	pet	pit
49	reed	rad	red	rid
50	bile	pile	file	vile
51	bine	pine	fine	vine
52	by	pie	phi	vie
53	seat	sat	set	sit
54	seed	sad	said	Sid
55	seen	san	sen	sin
56	sap	zap	jap	chap
57	Jew	chew	zoo	shoe
58	Joe	Cho	Zoh	show
59	lead	lad	led	lid
60	boor	poor	four	for

4

	1st	2nd	3rd	4th
61	noon	none	noun	known
62	Rhine	wine	nine	line
63	fool	full	foul	foal
64	link	rink	wink	
65	teen	tan	tin	
66	wheel	well	will	
67	lake	rake	wake	
68	letter	wetter	redder	
69	boom	bum	bomb	
70	goon	gun	gone	
71	lewd	rude	nude	
72	lice	rice	nice	
73	rail	nail	wail	
74	bro	pro	fro	
75	bit	fit	pit	
76	meal	Mell	mill	
77	leak	week	reek	
78	fear	beer	peer	
79	beat	peat	feet	
80	bill	pill	fill	

5 THIRD GROUP

	Left	Middle	Right
81	this	tis	dis
82	though	toe	doe
83	thought	sought	taught
84	threw	true	drew
85	thy	tie	die
86	them	Tim	dim
87	theme	team	deem
88	there	tear	dare
89	therm	term	derm
90	think	tink	dink
91	loom	room	womb
92	kneel	real	wheel
93	lair	rare	where
94	cab	cap	calf
95	hoot	hut	hot
96	swab	swap	suave
97	fork	park	pork
98	wrap	lap	nap
99	raid	Wade	laid
100	toon	ton	town

6

	Left	Middle	Right
101	lent	rent	went
102	new	rue	loo
103	leather	weather	nether
104	man	mean	men
105	batter	patter	fatter
106	lather	rather	
107	legal	regal	
108	loyal	royal	
109	rational	national	
110	billow	pillow	
111	boat	vote	
112	boil	foil	
113	brown	frown	
114	razor	laser	
115	poodle	puddle	
116	list	wrist	
117	spoon	spun	
118	lighter	writer	
119	liver	river	
120	slacker	snacker	

Top 40 Konglish Expressions

Here is a list of things that Americans do not say, but Koreans think they say.
These are not necessarily bad grammar; they are just not used by Americans, or are used differently.
For example, Americans seldom begin a sentence with "Especially."

	Americans do not say	**Americans really say**
1	almost (to mean "most"/"mostly")	most of, almost always, almost everywhere
2	arbeit	part-time job
3	Are you boring?	Are you bored?
4	CF	commercial
5	cunning	cheating
6	cut the film	can't remember, blacked out
7	DC	discount
8	eat medicine	take medicine
9	especially	(Don't begin a sentence with this word.)
10	eye shopping	browsing, window shopping
11	Fighting!	Do it! Go for it!
12	Frankly speaking	To be honest, Honestly, Frankly
13	high eyes	high standards, picky
14	How about your feelings?	How did you feel?
15	How about your weekend?	How was your weekend?
16	I envy you.	Wow! You lucky dog.
17	I have a plan this weekend.	I have plans this weekend.
18	I'm funny.	I'm having fun.
19	In my case, . . .	Just begin with *I* . . .
20	make a boyfriend or girlfriend	find / get a boyfriend or girlfriend
21	maul bus / village bus	shuttle bus
22	meeting	blind date
23	overeat	throw up
24	play with my friends	hang out with my friends
25	pocket money	allowance, spending money
26	said to me	told me
27	salaryman	(Americans say the exact job or industry.)
28	same to me, same to her	me too, her too
29	See you again!	See you later!
30	service	freebie, on the house, complimentary
31	She has princess disease.	She's stuck-up / conceited.
32	sign	*signature* or *autograph* ("Sign" is a verb.)
33	super	supermarket, convenience store
34	take a rest	take a break
35	talent	celebrity, actor, singer, MC, host
36	This is funny.	This is fun.
37	toilet	restroom
38	vinyl house	greenhouse
39	yesterday night	last night
40	yet	not yet

STOP saying these things.

10 DESCRIBING

1. mustache

2. balding, goatee

3. bald, beard

4. military cut

5. shaved head

6. shoulder-length, wavy, streaked hair

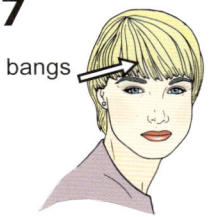
7. bangs and short, thin, straight hair

8. long, thick, wavy hair

9. frizzy hair

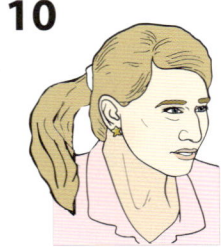
10. ponytail

1. He has straight hair, combed back and parted on the left. He is grinning, he has thick eyebrows, and he has a mustache. He is facing the right. He is wearing a coat and tie.
2. He is balding, and he has a goatee. He has wrinkles on his forehead and around his eyes. He is wearing a crewneck sweater.
3. He is bald, with black hair and a black beard. He is facing the right and smiling. He looks plump or even fat.
4. He has a dark complexion and a military haircut. He is wearing a V-neck shirt and he looks muscular.
5. He has a shaved head and a dark complexion. He's wearing a collared shirt, buttoned at the neck, but no tie.
6. She has shoulder-length, streaked hair that is parted slightly on the left. She is facing the left, and she has a serious expression.
7. She has short, thin, straight, light-colored hair and bangs. Her body is facing right, and her head is facing forward. She is wearing a collarless top.
8. She has long, thick, wavy dark-brown hair. She is facing the left, and she has long eyebrows. She has a mole on her cheek.
9. She has very thick, very frizzy long hair. She is smiling, and her face is kind of square. She has on big earrings and a low-cut V-neck top.
10. She has her long hair pulled back into a ponytail. She has a serious expression, and she is looking to the right. She has on a light-colored, collared top.

RECEDING HAIRLINE: Nicholas Cage, Tom Hanks
BALDING: Sean Connery, Gene Hackman, Bruce Willis
SALT & PEPPER (gray & black) **HAIR:** Richard Gere
STRONG JAW: Jay Leno
SQUARE FACE: Arnold Schwarzenegger
DIMPLES: Tom Cruise

polka dot

checkered

thin vertical stripes

thick horizontal stripes

diagonal stripes

plaid

paisley

 48

1. She has long, thin, straight hair and bangs. She is wearing a sheer (see-through) top over a white body stocking. She is wearing tight dress jeans and calf-length, soft leather boots.

2. She also has long, thin hair with bangs, but her hair is a little wavy. She's wearing jewelry: earrings, a necklace, and a white bracelet. She's wearing a loose-fitting, peasant-type top, which has elbow-length sleeves and is gathered at the waist. She has a diagonal-striped short skirt and sandal-type high heels with straps.

3. She has long, thick, jet-black hair, but not bangs. She's wearing a light open-neck sweater. She has a bare midriff, barely. She's wearing camouflage cargo pants and flat sandals.

4. She has thick, black hair that is parted on the left and gathered in back. She's wearing a long-sleeved top and tight, boot-cut dress jeans. (Boot-cut means the bottoms are flared out to fit over boots. Jeans usually come in straight-leg, boot-cut, flared, and bell-bottoms.) You can't see it, but her shoes are pumps, which means they are in between flats and high heels.

5. She's wearing a horizontal-striped, loose-fitting top with big, baggy short sleeves. She's wearing tight, calf-length blue jeans, and spiked high heels. (If her heels were a bit longer, they would be stiletto heels.)

6. She has thick black hair pulled back into a ponytail. She's wearing a low-cut sleeveless top, a knee-length print skirt, and sandals.

7. She has shoulder-length, thick brown hair and bangs. She's wearing a white leather jacket over a diagonal-striped top. She has on a blue jean mini-skirt, and she's wearing open-toed, medium-heeled shoes.

8. She has short, wavy hair. She's wearing a loose-fitting, short-sleeved top, a casual blue jean mini-skirt, and tennis shoes.

FEMALES

← FACING THE LEFT FACING THE RIGHT →

Descriptions p. 90

PLAN A:

1. Sit in a group of 3: A, B, and C.
2. A will secretly select a female and describe her.
   (A will be sneaky and hide her eyes, so that B and C cannot see where A is looking.)
3. B and C will guess who she is describing.
4. If B and C guess wrong, then they will ask questions to try to figure out who A is describing. They can use the questions below.
5. After they correctly guess A's model, it is B's turn. Then C's. Then A's again.
   Note: You could describe the person fully, and they could quickly guess the answer.
   Or you could give just a little information, to make them ask plenty of questions.

Example:

A She has shoulder-length, slightly wavy hair.
B Number 4! I win, I win!
A Wrong.
C Number 2! Number 2!
A Wrong.
B What color is her hair?
A She has light hair.
C Does she have bangs? Maybe number 23?
A No.
B Is she smiling?
A No.
C Is she happy or sad, young or old?
A She is not smiling, but she doesn't look sad. She looks about 30.
B Is her head leaning down toward the left, like number 32?
A No.
C What is she wearing?
A She has on a striped top with no collar.
B Are they horizontal or vertical stripes?
A Horizontal stripes.
C Number 12! Number 12!
A Du-uh! Those are vertical stripes. Relax. Breathe deeply.
B Which way is she facing?
A She's facing left.
B Number 14!
A FINALLY! Right.

HELPFUL QUESTIONS
Is she average, pretty, or beautiful?
Is her hair long or short? Straight or wavy?
Is her hair light or dark? Thick or thin?
Does she have bangs? Are they straight?
Is her hair pulled back or parted?
Which side is it parted on?
Does she have a high hairline?
Does she have a strong or weak jaw?
Which way is she facing?
Are her clothes dressy or casual?
Is she smiling or serious?
Is her hair wild or combed?
Is her top a turtleneck or low-cut?
Is she wearing any jewelry?

PLAN B:

Same as method 1, except that A does NOT describe her selection. B and C begin by asking questions, and A answers only with a YES or NO, or only one word.

Example:

B Is she young or old?
A Young.
C Does she have black hair?
A No.
B Does she have long hair?
A No.
C Does she have bangs?
A Yes.
B Is her hair straight or wavy?
C Curly.

(And so on.)

PLAN C:
Describe your favorite female movie stars, foreign or Korean. Your partners will ask questions and try to guess.

You can describe their looks, build, personality, the kind of movies they make, and the kind of characters they usually play.

Hey! You can do the same with your favorite singer.

MALES

← PARTED ON THE RIGHT   PARTED ON THE LEFT →

Descriptions p. 91

PLAN A:
Same as Plan A for the females.

Example:
- A He has short, thin hair and he is middle-aged or a little older.
- B Is he wearing a coat and tie?
- A No.
- C Is he wearing a coat?
- A No.
- B Is he wearing sunglasses?
- A No.
- C Does he have a mustache or a beard?
- A No.
- B Is he bald, or does he have a receding hairline?
- A Well, maybe not a receding hairline, but at least he has a high forehead.
- C Number 8!
- A No, his hair is not exactly thin.
- B Is he facing to the right or the left?
- A He is looking straight ahead.
- C Does he have a Chinese collar shirt? Number 30!
- A Wrong.
- C Is he wearing a sweater?
- A Yes.
- B Is it a solid color or does it have a polka dot or diamond-pattern design?
- A Solid color.
- B Number 12!
- A No. But close.
- C Wait, wait. Number 34 is the same as 12, except that their hair is parted on different sides. Is it number 34?
- A BINGO!

HELPFUL QUESTIONS
Is his hair long or short? Thick or thin?
Is his hair straight or wavy? Light or dark?
Is he going bald and trying to hide it?
Is his hair combed back or parted on the side?
Which side is his hair parted on?
Is he smiling or frowning?
Is he happy or serious?
Is he wearing a coat? Light or dark?
Is he wearing a tie?
Is he looking straight ahead or to the side?
Does he have a beard or mustache?
Is he dressed up or casual?
Can you see his teeth?
About how old is he?

PLAN B:
Same as method 1, except that A does NOT describe his/her selection. B and C begin by asking questions, and A answers only with a YES or NO, or only one word.

Example:
- B Is he young or old?
- A Young.
- C Is he smiling?
- A Yes.
- B Can you see his teeth?
- A No.
- C Does he have bangs?
- A Yes.
- B Are his eyebrows thick or average?
- C Thick.

(And so on.)

PLAN C:
Describe your favorite male movie stars, foreign or Korean. Your partners will ask questions and try to guess.

You can describe their looks, build, personality, the kind of movies they make, and the kind of characters they usually play.

Try it with your favorite male singer also.

DESCRIPTIONS: FEMALES

1. She has long, wavy blond hair, which is parted on the left. She is smiling and her body is slightly facing the left. She is wearing a collarless top.
2. She has shoulder-length, dark brown hair, and she is facing the right. She is smiling slightly and she is wearing a horizontal-striped top.
3. She has long, thick, wavy black hair that is pulled back out of her face. She has long eyebrows and a strong jaw. Her dark top has no collar.
4. She has long, thick, wild, uncombed hair, and bangs. She is smiling and she has a thick lips, a big mouth, and big teeth. She is wearing a V-neck top.
5. She has neck-length thick, wavy dark hair. She is smiling and looking slightly down. She is wearing a low-cut, sleeveless top. It looks like it could be an aerobics outfit.
6. She has long, wavy black hair that falls in front of her shoulders. She has dark eye makeup and she is facing the right.
7. She has long hair that she is wearing up. She has a serious expression, and she has on a V-neck top.
8. She has long, very thick, frizzy hair. She is smiling and wearing earrings. She has on a low-cut top.
9. She has short, straight dark hair that is parted on the left. She has high cheekbones and is wearing a black blouse or jacket.
10. She has short, thin, straight hair that is combed forward. She is smiling broadly and she is facing the left. She has big eyes and a big mouth. Her shirt has a really big collar.
11. She has short hair that is combed in a man's hairstyle. She has a serious expression, and she has a V-neck top.
12. Same as number 2, but with vertical stripes and blonde hair.
13. She has long, thick, wavy black hair that is pulled back from her face. She has long eyebrows and a strong jaw. She has a high forehead and her dark top has no collar.
14. Same as number 2, but with light hair and facing the left.
15. Same as number 4, but with no makeup on. Or maybe she has acne.
16. She has long, very thick, frizzy hair. She has a serious expression, and her head is leaning a little down and toward the left. Her top has no collar.
17. She has short, straight, dark hair that is combed forward. Maybe she is wearing heavy eye makeup. She is looking straight ahead.
18. She has long, thick, wavy blond hair. She is facing right. She is wearing a bikini top, or a spaghetti strap, very low-cut dress. It's called a spaghetti strap because it is very thin, like a strand of spaghetti. Her top shows cleavage.
19. She has short, curly blond hair. She has a serious expression and she is facing the right. Her top is collarless.
20. She has short, thick hair with heavy bangs. Her hair is thicker on top than it is on the sides. She is smiling and looking straight ahead. She is wearing a turtleneck top.
21. She has short dark hair that is combed forward. She has bangs, big eyes, and a strong jaw. She's wearing earrings and a collared top. She is facing the left.
22. She has short curly hair, with a longer lock of hair behind each ear. Those are called ringlets. She's not smiling or frowning and she is facing the front. Her top has no collar.
23. She looks positively perky! She has shoulder-length hair that curls out at the shoulders. She has even bangs. She has a big smile and is facing the right.
24. Same as number 2, but with light hair.
25. Same as number 1, but her hair is parted on the right, and her body is facing right.
26. She has a "pageboy" hairdo: short, shoulder-length hair that curls in at the shoulders, and bangs. She is facing directly forward and wearing a turtleneck top.
27. Same as number 8, but with a turtleneck top.
28. She has long blond hair that is brushed back out of her face. She is facing straight ahead and wearing a T-shirt.
29. She has long, thick, dark hair that is brushed back. She has a strong jaw and long eyebrows. She has a low hairline and she is facing the left.
30. The same as number 18, but she is facing left and has a blue and white geometric pattern top.
31. She has dark, shoulder-length hair and maybe a perm. She has a big smile and is wearing a T-shirt.
32. She has shoulder-length thick black hair with bangs. She has long eyebrows. She is facing the left and her head is tilted slightly down. She's smiling.
33. Same as number 6, but with a dark complexion.
34. She has an angular face and has shoulder-length, very wavy hair—not quite curly, but close. She has big earrings, and she is wearing a strapless dress.
35. Same as number 2, but with vertical stripes and facing left.

DESCRIPTIONS: MALES

1. He looks like an aging rock star. He has short, thick hair with bangs. His hair is longer in the back than in the front. He's wearing sunglasses, a horizontal striped T-shirt, and a dark jacket.
2. He looks like a light-skinned African American. He has short curly hair and a goatee. He is facing the left and his head is tilted slightly down. He has a high forehead and he's wearing a bowtie.
3. He has short, curly dark hair and a receding hairline. He is facing straight ahead. He is smiling and wearing a T-shirt.
4. He looks like an accountant. He has short, straight, thin hair that is parted on the left. He has a collared shirt under a crew-neck, diamond-patterned sweater. He's wearing thin-framed glasses.
5. He has long, wavy light-colored hair. He has a mustache and an intense expression on his face. He is facing the left, and he's wearing a light-colored T-shirt and a dark coat.
6. Same as number 5, but a with dark hair and a light coat.
7. He is kind of old, and he looks plump or even pudgy. He is bald with gray hair and a goatee. He's trying to smile and he's wearing a blue, casual, collared shirt. dark T-shirt.
8. He's 30 to 40 and has a big smile. He has short, dark hair that is combed back. His hair is thicker on top than it is on the sides. He's wearing a casual, collared shirt.
9. He has short, brown, slicked-backed hair. (If hair has gel or mousse in it, it is called slicked.) He's facing the left, but he's looking this way. He has long, thick eyebrows. He's wearing a suit, a coat, and tie.
10. He's an African American. Same as number 2, but with a darker complexion.
11. Same as number 9 but facing the right.
12. Same as number 4, but his hair is parted on the right, and his sweater is a solid color.
13. Same as number 11, but with gray hair.
14. He is old, and his hair is kind of long for an old man. His hair is white and parted on the right. He's wearing rimmed glasses. He has on a white dress shirt and tie, and a vertical-striped sweater vest.
15. He's a little old and going bald, but he combs his hair forward to try to hide the baldness. His hair is thick on the sides, and he has sideburns. He has thick eyebrows and wrinkles around his eyes. He has on a casual shirt and a plaid coat.
16. The same as number 1, but with a solid-colored T-shirt and a dark jacket.
17. He's a little older, with short dark hair. His hair is graying at the temples. (Often, when men's hair turns gray, it starts at the temples.) He's wearing a coat and tie.
18. The same as number 4, but wearing a polka dot sweater.
19. Same as number 1, but with a light-colored coat.
20. He's wearing thick-rimmed glasses. He has short dark hair. He's wearing an open-collared shirt and coat.
21. Same as number 6 but facing the right.
22. He's an African American with thick, very curly hair. If his hairdo was a little thicker, you would call that an "Afro." He's wearing a suit and smiling broadly.
23. He has a high forehead and a receding hairline. He has short dark hair, long sideburns, and thick eyebrows. He's wearing a casual, collared shirt.
24. He is bald, with a beard, and he looks heavy. He's wearing a camouflaged sweater, and he has a little gap between his top front teeth.
25. Same as number 6, but he's facing right and has on a dark T-shirt.
26. Same as number 24, but facing the right.
27. Same as number 5, but facing the right, with a light-colored coat.
28. Same as number 1, but with a checkered T-shirt.
29. Same as number 15, but with a checkered jacket.
30. He has light-colored hair that is combed back. He's wearing a Chinese collar shirt.
31. Same as number 22, but his hair is close-cropped (shorter).
32. Same as number 1, but with a diagonal-striped T-shirt.
33. He has a high forehead and receding hairline. (Often, when a man's hairline starts to recede, he will let his hair grow longer in the back, to sort of compensate. The general rule is: As it gets thinner on top, it gets longer in the back.) His hair is thicker on the sides and thinner on top. He's smiling and wearing an open-collared casual shirt.
34. Same as number 12, but his hair is parted on the left.
35. He has a strong jaw. He has salt-and-pepper hair. (Salt is gray and pepper is black, so salt-and-pepper hair is black and gray hair.) He is arching his eyebrows.

11 CORE VOCABULARY

LOOKS, HAIR, & BUILD

 49

FEMALE LOOKS

ugly	못생긴
unattractive; homely	매력 없는
plain	평범한
so-so	그저 그런, 보통의
fair	보통의 외모인
average	보통의
OK	외모가 괜찮은
cute	귀여운, 예쁜
good-looking	잘 생긴
pretty	예쁜
precious	가치 있는, 사랑스러운
beautiful	아름다운
gorgeous	매우 아름답고 멋진
stops traffic	매우 아름답고 근사한
drop-dead gorgeous	매우 멋지고 아름다운

MEN & WOMEN'S BUILD

(M = males only)

tall / short / medium	(키가) 큰, 작은, 중간인
thin / fat / average	날씬한 / 뚱뚱한 / 보통의
skin and bones	매우 마른
skinny	마른
slender	쭉 빠진
washboard stomach (M)	날씬한 배
muscular	근육질의
love handles (M)	아랫배의 군살
plump	통통한
pudgy	땅딸막한
stocky (M)	작고 단단한
heavy-set	체격 좋게 살찐
beer belly (M)	술배
obese	비만

WOMEN'S BUILD

voluptuous	가슴이 매우 큰 매력적인 몸매
hour-glass figure	허리가 잘록한 몸매
fine	멋진
long legs; legs up to here	긴 다리
plump	통통한
pleasingly plump	귀엽게 포동포동한

MALE LOOKS

ugly	못생긴
unattractive; homely	매력적이지 않은
plain	평범한
so-so	그저그런, 보통의
fair	보통의 외모인
average	보통의
OK	괜찮은 외모의
cute	귀여운
good-looking	잘생긴
pretty boy	예쁘게 생긴 남자
ruggedly handsome	전체적으로 괜찮게 잘 생긴
handsome	매우 잘 생긴
(well-)built	몸짱

MEN'S HAIR

beard	턱수염
goatee	염소수염 (턱 밑)
mustache	콧수염 (Clark Gable)
sideburns	구레나룻 (Elvis)
hairy chest	가슴에 털이 있는
receding hairline	앞머리부터 빠져가는

WOMEN'S HAIR

bangs	짧게 자른 앞머리
colored; dyed	염색한
streaked	줄무늬 염색 (브릿지)
wavy	약간 부드럽게 곱슬거리는
curly	곱슬곱슬한
permed	파마한
frizzy	매우 곱슬거리는
pigtails	땋아늘인 머리 (양쪽)
ponytail	한가닥을 뒤로 묶은 머리
pulled back	뒤로 싹 넘겨 묶은 머리
parted in the middle	앞가르마의
in a bun	올린 머리

SKIN

silky-smooth	부드럽고 매끈한
like a baby's bottom	보드라운
soft, smooth	폭신한, 부드러운
milky-white	우유처럼 하얀
weathered	거칠고 햇볕에 탄
leathery	거친, 가죽처럼 질긴
acne; pitted; scarred	자국이 남은
wrinkled	주름진

CLOTHES

PANTS
baggy	헐렁한, 불룩한
straight leg	상하 넓이가 같은 일자 바지
boot-cut	아래통이 넓은 바지
flared	밑이 넓은 바지 / 스커트
bell-bottoms	나팔바지
shorts	반바지
cut-offs	무릎에서 자른 청바지
knee-length pants	무릎 길이의 바지
button-fly	지퍼 대신 단추로 된 바지

SKIRTS & DRESSES
pleated	주름진
ankle-length	발목까지 오는
calf-length	종아리까지 오는
knee-length	무릎까지 오는
miniskirt	미니 스커트
wrap-around skirt	허리에 두르는 스커트
slit skirt	옆트임 치마
mini-dress	미니 드레스

TOPS
stripes: wide / thin	줄무늬: 넓은 것 / 가는 것
horizontal stripe	가로줄 무늬
vertical stripe	세로줄 무늬
bare midriff	배꼽티
checkered	체크 무늬
flowered	꽃 무늬
halter top	등이 많이 드러나는 옷
long-sleeved	긴 소매
low-cut	목이 깊게 파인 옷
print, pattern	그림이나 문양이 있는 옷
short-sleeved	짧은 소매
sleeveless	소매가 없는
spaghetti strap	가는 어깨끈으로 된 것
turtleneck	목을 감싸는 폴라
V-neck	목이 V모양으로 된 것
backless dress	등이 많이 파인 드레스
tank top	탱크톱
pajamas (PJ's)	파자마 (원피스 잠옷)
pantyhose	팬티 스타킹
scarf	스카프
slip / full slip	슬립 / 속치마
stockings	스타킹
lingerie	디자인을 강조한 여성용 잠옷
underwear; undergarments	속옷
panties (for women)	여성팬티
one-piece swimsuit	(원피스) 수영복
bikini; two-piece	비키니
stained	얼룩진, 더러운 것이 묻은
ripped; torn	부분적으로 찢어진
shrink; shrunk	(잘못 세탁해서) 줄어든
pre-shrunk	줄어드는 것을 방지한

"This is too . . ."
tight	몸에 꽉 끼는	loose	느슨한, 성긴
light	밝은	dark	어두운, 칙칙한
bright	(빛깔이) 선명한, 산뜻한		
loud	요란한 (빛깔)		
thick	두꺼운		
thin	얇은		
sheer	얇은, 비치는		
risqué; sexy	섹시한; 야한		
out of style	유행에 뒤져있는		
old-fashioned	구식의, 유행에 뒤져있는		
tacky	초라한, 볼품없는		

"This material is kind of . . ."
soft	부드러운, 매끈매끈한
hard	딱딱한, 견고한, 튼튼한
rough	거칠한, (털이) 헝클어진
smooth	매끄러운
wrinkled	주름진
wet	젖은, 축축한
dirty	지저분한
filthy	더러운, 불결한
smelly	(고약한) 냄새나는

MATERIAL
fur / fake fur	모피 / 인조가죽		
leather	가죽		
polyester	폴리에스터		
polyester blend	폴리에스터 합성섬유		
cotton	면	silk	비단
velvet	우단	wool	모

MEN'S STUFF
button-down collar	셔츠깃 끝을 단추로 고정
dress shirt	정장 셔츠
polo shirt	스포츠 셔츠
muscle shirt	소매가 없는 셔츠
jersey	운동선수복의 상의 (축구, 럭비)
suspenders	멜빵
belt	벨트
cargo pants	주머니가 많은 작업용바지
permanent press	구김을 방지하는 영구가공
wrinkle-free	구김이 잘 생기지 않는

SUITS
two- / three-button	단추가 2개 / 3개 있는 양복상의
single-breasted	양복상의가 겹치지 않게 입는
double-breasted	양복상의가 겹치게 입는
blazer	단체복 상의의 일종

COATS
bomber jacket	항공 점퍼, 군용 재킷
trench coat	트렌치 코트 (바바리)
windbreaker	방한, 방풍용의 스포츠재킷

SHOES
tennis	테니스화
dress	정장화
jogging	조깅화
platform	굽이 두꺼운 캐주얼화

FOOTWEAR
pumps	굽이 약간 있는 신발	high heels	하이힐
		flats	굽이 낮은 신발
sandals	샌달		
hiking boots	등산화	slippers	슬리퍼

ACCESSORIES
bracelet	팔찌	necklace	목걸이
brooch	브로치	purse	여성지갑
handbag	핸드백	wallet	남성지갑

JOBS

1	accountant	회계사
2	actor / actress	남자배우 / 여배우
3	anchorman / anchorwoman	남자앵커 / 여자앵커
4	artist	예술가
5	attorney	변호사
6	banker	은행원
7	bartender	바텐더
8	businessman	벽돌공
9	CEO	사업가
10	chauffeur	자가용운전사
11	chef	최고경영자
12	clerk: bank / post office	사무원(은행,우체국)
13	computer graphics designer	컴퓨터 그래픽 디자이너
14	computer programmer	컴퓨터 프로그래머
15	construction worker	공사장 인부
16	dancer	무용가, 댄서
17	dentist	치과의사
18	detective	형사
19	diplomat	외교관
20	director / producer	감독 / 제작자
21	doctor	의사
22	electrician	전기공
23	engineer	기술자
24	entrepreneur	사업가
25	farmer	농부
26	firefighter	소방관
27	hairstylist	미용사
28	interior decorator	실내장식가
29	interpreter	통역사
30	journalist	신문잡지 기자
31	judge	판사
32	lawyer	변호사
33	librarian	사서
34	mailman	집배원
35	military officer / soldier	군인
36	minister; pastor	성직자, 외교관, 장관, 목사
37	monk	승려, 수사
38	nurse	간호사
39	pilot	조종사
40	plumber	배관공
41	politician	정치가
42	priest	카톨릭 신부
43	reporter	리포터
44	salesclerk	판매원
45	salesperson	판매원
46	scientist	과학자
47	secretary	비서
48	self-employed	자영업의
49	stewardess; flight attendant	여자 승무원, 남자 승무원
50	surgeon	외과의사
51	tailor	재단사
52	truck driver	트럭 운전사
53	blue-collar worker	노무직 종사자
54	white-collar worker	사무직 종사자

MAJORS

Accounting	회계학
Advertising	광고학
Agriculture	농학
Agronomy	농업경제학
Architecture	건축학
Art	예술전공
Art History	예술사
Biology	생물학
Business Administration	경영학
Chemical Engineering	화학공학
Chemistry	화학
Chinese	중국어
Computer Graphics	컴퓨터그래픽
Dance	무용
Drama	연극영화
Economics	경제학
Electrical Engineering	전기공학
Engineering	공학, 기관학
Environmental Science	환경과학
Fashion Design	의상디자인
Fine Arts	순수미술
Food & Nutrition	식품경영학
General Business	일반 경영학
Geography	지질학
Health Science	보건학
Herbal (Chinese) Medicine	한의학
History	역사
Info. & Comm. Technology	정보통신기술학
Interior Design	실내장식
Japanese	일본어
Law	법학
Library & Information Science	문헌정보학
Life Science	생명과학
Mathematics	수학
Mechanical Engineering	기계공학
Medicine	의학도(의과대생)
Music	음악
Natural Science	자연과학
Nursing	간호학
Pharmacy	약학
Philosophy	철학
Physics	물리학
Psychology	심리학
Public Administration	행정학
Radio & TV Broadcasting	방송학
Safety Engineering	안전공학
Theology	신학
Tourism	관광학과
Urban Planning	도시계획
Zoology	동물학
graduate school	대학원
humanities	인문학부
social sciences	사회학부
liberal arts	교양학부

PERSONALITY ACRONYMS

 53    54

1	absent-minded	건망증이 있는
2	adorable	존경할 만한, 사랑스러운
3	ambitious	야망 있는
4	artistic	미적감각이 있는
5	blunt	무딘, 무뚝뚝한
6	bossy	남을 다스리고자 하는
7	charismatic	카리스마적인
8	clever	영리한
9	closed- / open-minded	옹졸한 / 편견 없는
10	compassionate	동정을 많이 주는
11	conformist	반항적인 사람
12	conservative	보수주의자
13	considerate	사려 깊은
14	cooperative	협동적인
15	creative	창조적인
16	creepy	소름끼치는
17	demure	차분한, 얌전한
18	diplomatic	외교적인
19	disgusting	구역질 나는, 꼴불견의
20	easygoing	편안한 성격의
21	gracious	자비로운, 인자한
22	gregarious	사교적인
23	grouchy	토라진
24	hyper	몹시 흥분한
25	immature	미숙한
26	impulsive	충동적인
27	insecure	믿을 수 없는
28	intellectual	지적인
29	intolerant	완고한
30	irresponsible	무책임한
31	laid-back	느긋한
32	loyal	충실한
33	mean	비열한, 못된
34	mellow	원만한
35	mild-mannered	온순한
36	mischievous	장난을 좋아하는
37	moody	우울한
38	narrow-minded	마음이 좁은
39	nonconformist	관행을 따르지 않는 사람
40	obnoxious	역겨운
41	optimistic	낙천주의의
42	passionate	열정적인
44	pessimistic	비관적인
45	secretive	비밀스런
46	self-confident	자신만만한
47	selfish	이기적인
48	sensitive	섬세한
49	spoiled	버릇 없는
50	stubborn	완고한
51	sweet	상냥한
52	temperamental	변덕스러운
53	tolerant	인내심이 강한
54	troublemaker	문제아, 말썽꾸러기
55	well-informed	박식한

AKA	also known as
ASAP	as soon as possible
BYOB	bring your own beer
CEO	chief executive officer
CIA	Central Intelligence Agency
DUI	driving under the influence
DWI	driving while intoxicated
FBI	Federal Bureau of Investigation
FDA	Food & Drug Administration
FYI	for your information
GPA	grade point average
ID	identification
IOU	"I owe you" (a debt)
IRS	Internal Revenue Service
MBA	Master's of Business Administration.
MLB	Major League Baseball
NATO	North Atlantic Treaty Organization
P.S.	postscript
RSVP	*Respondez s'il vous plait.* (Please respond to the invitation.)
SOS	save our ship (a call for help)
TGIF	thank goodness it's Friday
UFO	unidentified flying object
UN	United Nations
VIP	very important person

EDUCATION

GMAT	Graduate Management Admission Test
GRE	Graduate Record Exam
LSAT	Law School Admission Test
TOEIC	Test of English for International Communication
TOEFL	Test of English as a Foreign Language

DEGREES

BA / BS	Bachelor of Arts / Science
MA / MS	Master of Arts / Science
ABD	all but dissertation (almost a PhD)
PhD	doctor of philosophy

MILITARY

AWOL	absent without leave
MIA / KIA	missing in action / killed in action
POW	prisoner of war

CHATTING

BFF	best friends forever
BRB	be right back
JK	just kidding
LOL	laughing out loud
NP	no problem
OMG	oh my gosh!
RT	retweet
SMH	shaking my head
TMI	too much information
TTYL	talk to you later
YOLO	you only live once

12 CORE SKILLS

 55

HOW OFTEN?
all the time
always
almost always
as often as possible
every chance I get
most of the time
frequently
often
regularly
usually
generally
normally
sometimes
occasionally
on occasion
every now and then
on special occasions
not too often
seldom
rarely
very seldom
hardly ever
once in a blue moon
never
never ever
when pigs fly

FREQUENCY
once a day / week / month / year
twice a day / week / month / year
three times a day / week / month / year
four times a day / week / month / year
every other day / week / month / year

PASSAGE OF TIME
ten years / months / days ago
the day before yesterday
last night
this morning
today
this afternoon
this evening
tonight
tomorrow
tomorrow morning / afternoon / night
the day after tomorrow
next week / month / year
in two days / weeks / months / years

QUALITY
awesome
magnificent
fantastic
superb
wonderful
fabulous
excellent
outstanding
very good
great
pretty good
good
OK; fair; so-so
mediocre
It will do.
no smash hit
You didn't miss a thing.
poor
bad
pretty bad
lame
awful
terrible
horrible
the pits
It stank.

LIKES TO DISLIKES

1. I adore Brad Pitt.
2. I really love to travel.
3. I love going to nightclubs.
4. I enjoy cooking.
5. I like shopping in Apkujeong.
6. I don't mind taking the bus.
7. I don't care for diet cola.
8. I don't like to study all night.
9. I really don't like to wake up early.
10. I hate rude people.
11. I can't stand people who lie.
12. I detest arrogant people.

BODY PARTS

hair	머리카락	cheeks	볼	shoulder	어깨	throat	목구멍	bladder	방광
scalp	두피	dimples	보조개	armpit	겨드랑이	chest	흉부	buttocks	궁둥이의
skin	피부	mouth	입	arm	팔	heart	심장	butt	엉덩이
brain	뇌	tooth / teeth	치아	elbow	팔꿈치	lungs	폐	thigh	허벅다리
forehead	이마	gums	잇몸	forearm	팔뚝	ribs	늑골	knee	무릎
eyebrows	눈썹	tongue	혀	wrist	손목	stomach	위	calf	종아리
eyelashes	속눈썹	tonsils	편도선	palm	손바닥	liver	간장	shin	정강이
eyes	눈	chin	턱끝	thumb	엄지	kidney	신장	ankle	발목
nose	코	jaw	아래턱	finger	손가락	intestines	장	foot / feet	발
nostrils	콧구멍	neck	목	knuckle	손가락 마디	waist	허리	toes	발가락

FREQUENCY

Knowing how to talk about frequency is very important. It indicates your English skill level. For example, an English interview might begin with an easy question: "Do you have a hobby?" If you answer, "Yes, I play the piano," then you might be asked, "How often do you play the piano?" Your English level can then be determined by how you answer.

"Three times a week" indicates good English skill.
"Three a week" indicates a lower level of skill.

To be precise and clear when answering a frequency question, especially to someone of another culture, you should never answer with just "often" or "frequently." How often is "often"?

One person's "often" might be **once a week**, and another's might be **once a month**. Therefore, when answering a "how often" question, answer it using two expressions of frequency.

For example:

> How often do you see your grandmother? Pretty often, about once a week.
> I go to the movies every now and then, about once every two months.
> We get Chinese food delivered very seldom, maybe once every three months.
> I go to a coffee shop as often as possible, about four times a week.
> I exercise once in blue moon. Maybe once a year.
> I seldom drink, maybe about three times a year.

Note: usually, generally, and normally are used interchangeably. For example,
I usually wake up at 10. I generally wake up at 10. I normally wake up at 10.

QUALITY

You could probably describe quality with only these expressions: good, bad, very, and so-so.
My vacation was very good / good / so-so / bad / very bad.
This would mean that your English is so-so. So let's fix that.

The previous page contains twenty-six words to express that something was good or bad. The words go from best at the top, to worst at the bottom. A few of the expressions require their own structure, so here are some examples.

> My blind date was awesome.
> My vacation was magnificent / fantastic / superb / wonderful / fabulous / excellent / outstanding / very good / great / pretty good / OK / fair / so-so / mediocre.
> How was the new restaurant?
> It will do. It was no smash hit. It was poor / bad / pretty bad / lame / awful / terrible / horrible.
> How was the party?
> It was the pits.
> It stank.

TIME

THIS WEEKEND, NEXT WEEKEND:

On Monday, Tuesday, or Wednesday, if you say, "Next weekend, I will visit my hometown," you mean the coming weekend, a few days later.

But on Thursday or Friday, if you say, "Next weekend, I will visit my hometown," you mean the following weekend, eight or nine days later.

COMPARISON HELP

Rule 1   One-syllable words, such as big, tall, fast, smart
- My car is **bigger** than yours.
- My father is **taller** than yours.
- My computer is **faster** than yours.
- My dog is **smarter** than yours.

Rule 2   Two-syllable words that end in "y," such as pretty, dirty, curly, funny
- My sister is **prettier** than yours.
- Your blue jeans are **dirtier** than mine.
- My hair is **curlier** than yours.
- *Dumb and Dumber* was **funnier** than *Charlie's Angels*.

Rule 3   Two-syllable words, such as handsome, polite, clever, selfish
- My boyfriend is **more handsome** than yours.
- My mother is **more polite** than yours.
- My brother is **more clever** than yours.
- Your sister is **more selfish** than mine.

Rule 4   Three (or more)-syllable words, such as beautiful, intelligent, horrible, traditional
- My dress is **more beautiful** than yours.
- My pure breed dog is **more intelligent** than your mutt.
- My blind date was **more horrible** than yours.
- My grandfather is **more traditional** than yours.

Here, try a few.

My boyfriend
My favorite singer
My cell phone
My winter coat
My computer
My class schedule
My bedroom

🎧 56   SOME COMMON OPPOSITES

큰	big	small	작은	좋은	good	bad	나쁜	똑똑한	smart	dumb	멍청한
밝은	bright	dim	흐릿한	우아한	graceful	awkward	서투른	매끄러운	smooth	rough	거친
깨끗한	clean	dirty	더러운	높은	high	low	낮은	부드러운	soft	hard	딱딱한
깊은	deep	shallow	얕은	뜨거운	hot	cold	차가운	자극적인	spicy	bland	자극 없는
쉬운	easy	difficult	어려운	밝은	light	dark	어두운	강한	strong	weak	약한
먼	far	near	가까이	정돈된	neat	dirty	지저분한	키가 큰	tall	short	키가 작은
빠른	fast	slow	느린	예의 바른	polite	rude	버릇 없는	두꺼운	thick	thin	얇은
뚱뚱한	fat	skinny	깡마른	부유한	rich	poor	가난한	넓은	wide	narrow	좁은
평평한	flat	bumpy	울퉁불퉁한	날카로운	sharp	dull	무딘	어린, 젊은	young	old	나이 든, 늙은

13 EXPLANATIONS & EXAMPLES

PERSONALITY OPPOSITES (from p. 16)		100
Unit 1	FAMILY	103
Unit 2	HOBBIES & INTERESTS	104
Unit 3	UNIVERSITY	105
Unit 4	SHOPPING	109
Unit 5	MOVIES	111
Unit 6	FOOD & RESTAURANTS	114
Unit 7	SPORTS & EXERCISE	117
Unit 8	VACATIONS & TRAVEL	120

PERSONALITY OPPOSITES (from page 16)

outgoing: not shy. A synonym is "extroverted."
Jill is so outgoing. She makes friends in minutes.
shy: reserved, quiet. A synonym is "introverted."
I was shy when I first got to college. Jack is shy until he gets to know you.

- **morning person:** someone who is at their best and most productive in the morning
    I'm a morning person. I cannot study after 5 p.m.
    My father's a morning person. He wakes up at 5 every day and plays badminton before breakfast.
- **evening person:** someone who is at their best and most productive in the evening
    I'm an evening person. I don't come alive until after noon. While in graduate school, I became an evening person.
    I'd study until 2 or 3 a.m. and sleep till noon.

indoor person: someone who prefers to be indoors. They like to do indoor activities, such as watching TV, reading a book, surfing the Internet.
I'm an indoor person. I rarely leave home on the weekend.
outdoors person: someone who likes the outdoors.
My father is an outdoor person. He loves mountain climbing, jogging, and tennis.

- **joiner:** someone who joins many clubs and likes to belong to groups; a people person
    I wasn't a joiner until I went to college. Now I belong to three clubs.
- **loner:** someone who likes, or does not mind, being alone. Very shy people are often loners.
    I've always been kind of a loner. Give me a good book and a soft sofa, and I am happy.

messy, a mess: not neat or tidy. Their house, room, or desk is disorganized and, a little dirty.
Is your room always this messy? Your room is a mess. Please clean it up.
neat: organized, with everything in its proper place
How do you keep your desk so neat and clean?
clean freak; neat freak: someone who is excessively clean
My mother is a neat freak. She cleans the house twice a day. She even irons my father's socks.
tidy: very neat and orderly. If someone says, "I am not a clean freak, but I like things tidy," they ARE a clean freak.
slob: someone who is very messy
My brother is a slob. There are things growing in his room. He hasn't cleaned his room in two years.

- **punctual:** on time. *I am always punctual. I hate being late. My major professor is too punctual. His classes begin on time, and not one minute later.*
- **late:** not on time. *If you are late one more time, we are through. Being late is rude. Get here on time.*

have patience: not get upset easily or quickly
My mother has a lot of patience; she never gets upset.
I used to have patience, but the older I get, the less patience I have.
have a short fuse: get angry very easily and quickly. A bomb with a long fuse (thirty minutes) takes a long time to explode. A bomb with a short fuse (ten seconds) explodes very quickly.
Our taxi driver had a short fuse. He blew the horn and yelled at every red light. My professor is a nice guy, but he has a short fuse for cell phones in class.

- **polite:** well-mannered. *Jane is such a polite child. It was very polite of you to give that elderly woman a seat.*
- **rude:** impolite. *Why were you rude to the waitress? It wasn't her fault.*

couch potato: someone who sits on a sofa all day reading or watching TV
   I was a couch potato last weekend. I watched TV from Friday night to Sunday morning.
active; energetic: always doing something. *You are so active. Where do you get your energy?*
always on the go: active, always doing something, always in motion
   Jill is always on the go. She's either shopping or playing tennis, or helping at church, or cleaning her house. I get tired just talking to her.

big spender: someone who spends a lot of money and buys expensive things. They might be really rich, or they can spend more money than they can afford.
   My uncle is a big spender. He has an expensive car and clothes and he always pays whenever the whole family goes out to eat.
cheap: not liking to spend money
   He is very cheap. He would rather walk two miles than take a taxi. My husband is too cheap. For our anniversary, he took me out to eat at Burger King.
cheapskate: also means cheap, but is not as polite
   That man's a cheapskate; he never leaves a tip.
tightwad: also means cheap, but is a little more polite than *cheapskate*
   Come on, don't be such a tightwad. Buy it for your wife.

generous; unselfish; giving: happy to give their money, time, or talents
   My boss is generous. He is a generous person.
   My brother is generous with his time and talents. He coaches little league baseball for free.
stingy: wanting all or most of something, while others have little or nothing. If you win a million dollars in the lottery, and you give your unemployed brother ten dollars, you are stingy.
   Don't be so stingy. Stop being stingy.
   He had 100 cookies and he would not give you one? That is stingy.
selfish: wanting to have a lot, while others have only a little. For example, if your older brother had five new toys, and he would not let you play with any of them, he is selfish.
   Stop being selfish and share your ice cream with your brother.

early bird: someone who gets up early
   My father is an early bird. He's up at 5:00 every morning and jogs three miles before breakfast.
night owl: someone who stays up very late.
   My sister is a night owl. She stays up until about 4:00 a.m. every night. On the weekends, she's a night owl. The sun is up before she gets home.

party animal: someone who likes to stay out late and party
   Bill was a party animal right after he got out of the army. Wow! Jack is a party animal, but he is so shy at work. Those engineering majors are a bunch of party animals. They study hard and drink hard.
party pooper: someone who wants to go home early from the party; someone who does not want to party
   "Pooped" is slang for tired, exhausted.
   It's only 10 o'clock! Don't be such a party- pooper.
   My date was a party pooper. Just when things were getting started, she wanted me to bring her home.

honest, honest to a fault: truthful. Too honest. Perhaps you should tell a little lie rather than be so honest.
   He's honest to a fault. He should lie or at least learn to be a little more diplomatic.
tell white lies: to tell mall, innocent, harmless lies that allow you to be polite
   How do you like my new hairdo? Very attractive.
   Do you think I'll get into Harvard? Of course.
   How was my singing? Amazing! (Amazingly bad)
   How long before we get there? Only twenty more minutes.

modern: up-to-date in their thinking
My parents are pretty modern.
traditional: old-fashioned in their thinking
My parents are traditional. They don't approve of couples kissing or holding hands in public.

keep a secret: to keep private information private
Can you keep a secret? Do you blabber all over town? Don't tell Britney. She cannot keep a secret.
blabbermouth: someone who talks too much about things that should be kept secret
You blabbermouth. Why did you tell the boss you saw me at the mall after I called in sick? She's a blabbermouth. Do not tell her or she'll repeat it.
gossip: someone who talks about other people. Sometimes it's true and, sometimes not, but either way, they talk too much about other people. And often, what they are talking about is a secret, or should be.
Mary is a gossip. Don't tell her anything.
There was some gossip in the office about the boss's new secretary.
tattletale: similar to "blabbermouth," but more often used with children
Honey, play nice and don't be such a tattletale.
I could never get away with anything bad when I was a child. My brothers were tattletales.

well-organized: organized, well
My father is well- organized. His desk is always neat and tidy, he is never late, and he always knows where everything is.
have your act together: to be well-organized, to know what you are doing, to be competent
Wow. Our new professor has his act together. He really knows what he's doing.
That computer salesman had his act together.
disorganized: some people are usually neat, tidy, and well-organized. Some other people are disorganized. They are not neat, they can never find anything, like car keys. They are often late, and they often lose things.
You are so disorganized! How do you ever get anything done? I'm just too disorganized. By the time I found my book, I was too sleepy to study.
scatterbrained: a little worse than disorganized
"Do you realize that you're wearing one black and one brown shoe?" "Oops. I get very scatterbrained during finals."

modest; aw, shucks: shy, not boastful. "Aw, shucks" is something that a modest person might say when they are being praised.
"Wow. You saved that whole family from drowning!" "Aw, shucks, it was nothing. Anybody else would have done the same thing."
stuck-up; conceited; vain: having a high opinion of themselves
I don't like her, her; she's stuck-up. She's vain. Who's the stuck-up girl in the red dress?
Who's the conceited guy in the gray suit?

weekend warrior: a person who parties very heavily, but only on the weekend. A typical weekend warrior might be a student or businessman who studies or works hard during the week, then parties hard on Friday and Saturday night. *Bill's a weekend warrior; you should have seen him last night dancing on the bar.*
I was a weekend warrior in college, but not these days.
social drinker: someone who rarely drinks, usually only on social occasions such as weddings
(When Koreans say "social drinker" they mean a person who drinks socially, regularly.)
"Do you like to drink?" "Not really, I'm more of a social drinker. When my friends drink, I usually just have one beer and sip it all night."
My sister is a social drinker. She drinks every now and then, but never very much. Usually only at weddings.
teetotaler: someone who never drinks
My mother is a teetotaler.
"How was your date?" "Kind of a waste of money. The party had free booze, but she was a teetotaler."

lenient: permissive, easygoing, forgiving. *My father is pretty lenient. I can come home whenever.*
strict: harsh, severe, unforgiving. *My mother is strict. I must be home by 9 p.m. every night, even on weekends.*

1 FAMILY

age gap: the difference in age between two people
There is a five-year age gap between my sister and me. She is 26, and I am 21.

allowance: money given to children from their parents on a weekly or monthly basis
My parents give me $50 a week for my allowance.

ancestors: relatives who lived in the past, such as great-great-grandparents
My ancestors came from Italy. My ancestors used to own most of that province.

birth order: the chronological (by time) order, or sequence in which the children in one family are born
"What is the birth order in your family?" "I was born first, then my sister, and my brother last."

black sheep of the family: a family member whose character is very different (often embarrassingly different) from the rest of the family
My uncle is the black sheep of the family. He has been married four times, and he was arrested for robbery twice.

born and raised in: an idiomatic expression that means one was born and grew up in a certain place
I was born and raised in New Orleans, Louisiana.

close, close to: having strong emotional ties
She and her sister are very close. They do everything together.

cousin: a child of one's parent's brother or sister
I like Christmas because I get to see all my cousins.

descendants: relatives in a direct line that come from an individual, such as children, grandchildren, and great-grandchildren
Her great-grandfather bought a huge farm. Now, all his descendants own part of it.

distant relative: a relative not closely related
I know he's my distant relative, but I forgot how we are related.

divorce: a legal end to a marriage
She was surprised when her parents decided to get a divorce after thirty years of marriage.

extended family: includes all family members, as opposed to the immediate family, which includes just the parents and children
I usually get to see my extended family at Thanksgiving and Christmas.

family feud: a long-standing argument or hostility between two different families or different members within the same family
My dad and his brother are having a family feud because they both want my grandfather's farm.

far-flung: refers to many members of a family living long distances from one another
I live in Seoul. My sister lives in Singapore. My parents live in San Francisco. My family is really far-flung.

funeral: a ceremony held in honor of someone who died
Uncle John's funeral will be on Wednesday at St. Peter's.

grave: a place in which a person's body is buried after death
We visit the grave of my grandfather every year on the anniversary of his death.

hometown: the city or town where one was born and raised
She's very proud of her hometown and always talks about it.

inherit: to receive something from a relative after that relative dies
When my grandfather died, I inherited a lot of money from him.

inheritance: something received from a relative after that relative has died
She spent all her inheritance money during one day of shopping in Myeong-dong.

jealous: feeling envious towards someone
I don't understand why people are jealous of others. Why can't they be happy with what they have?

lenient: not strict about enforcing rules; easygoing
My parents are quite lenient. As long as my school grades are high, I can do whatever I want.

military family: a family in which one or both parents are in the military
I grew up in a military family, so I have lived in many places, like Germany and Korea.

only child: a person with no siblings
My wife is an only child, but sometimes she wishes she had grown up with a younger sibling.

originally from: used to indicate the place where someone was born before moving to another location
Now, I live in Seoul, but I am originally from Jejudo.

passed away: a gentle way of saying "died"
Everyone was shocked when she passed away, because she was in good health and was always active.

personal: relating to a particular person; private
You should never ask an adult about his or her age. That is personal information.

punish, punishment: to give a penalty because of bad behavior; the penalty is called the "punishment"
I agree that she should have been punished for cheating on her test; however, I believe the punishment was too harsh.

quality time: special time spent with close friends or family
Although he is always busy with work, he does try to spend some quality time with his children very weekend.

relative: family member such as a cousin, aunt, uncle, etc.
A lot of my relatives are coming to my house for my mom's birthday party.

religious family: a family that believes strongly in a religion and often practices that religion
She grew up in a very religious family. They went to the temple every weekend.

scandal: an infamous act or condition that could be embarrassing to some family members
My sister caused a scandal when she married one of her students; he was ten years younger than she was.

sibling: brother or sister
I have two siblings, an older brother and a younger sister.

spoiled brat: a child with bad, selfish behavior
I hate it when those two cousins visit. They are both such spoiled brats.

strict: using much discipline
My father is strict. I have to be home by 9 p.m. every night.

supportive: helping and encouraging; describes parents who provide emotional support for their children's choices in life
My parents are very supportive. They even helped me when I decided to change my major to archaeology.

take after; favor: to resemble, either physically or in personality
She takes after her mother. They are both pretty and are great cooks.

2 HOBBIES & INTERESTS

(Since students already know most of these hobbies, only example sentences are provided.)

aerobics: *Aerobics instructors have to be in great shape.*

astronomy: *The boy got a telescope for his birthday because he was interested in astronomy.*

badminton: *Badminton is a popular backyard sport.*

bicycle riding: *We like to go bicycle riding in the park on Sunday afternoons.*

billiards; pool: *I enjoy playing pool occasionally, but I don't understand the rules for billiards.*

bowling: *The kids all went bowling because it was Jeffrey's birthday.*

calligraphy: *The students practice calligraphy using special pens and high-quality paper.*

camping: *Having a good tent is essential for camping.*

computer games: *The boy's mother told him he couldn't play computer games until he finished his homework.*

cooking: *Cooking spaghetti is easy. Just boil the noodles and heat up the sauce, and then it's ready!*

crossword puzzles: *Doing a crossword puzzle is a good way to pass the time when flying on an airplane.*

dancing: *Although it takes on many different forms, dancing is one activity that nearly all cultures have in common.*

drawing: *She got in trouble for drawing pictures in the back of her textbook.*

fishing: *We spent all afternoon fishing and caught seven fish.*

golf: *My mother loves to golf; she says it really helps her deal with stress.*

hiking: *Hiking is a great way to exercise and enjoy the outdoors.*

martial arts: *Many action movie stars are trained in a variety of martial arts.*

mountain climbing: *Mountain climbing can be dangerous if climbers are not careful.*

musical instrument: *Learning to master a musical instrument takes lots of time, patience, and practice.*

painting: *Last week, I saw an artist painting a giant mural on the side of a downtown building.*

photography: *The invention of the digital camera revolutionized photography.*

ping pong: *I like ping pong more than tennis because players don't have to run!*

reading: *Reading is a great way to build up one's vocabulary.*

rollerblading: *The park is full of people rollerblading when the weather is nice.*

scuba diving: exploring underwater for extended periods with the aid of a mask and oxygen tank
The highlight of my trip to Thailand was scuba diving off the coast of Phi Phi Island.

sewing: using a needle and thread to make clothes
The women in my family have been sewing their own clothes for hundreds of years.

shoot pool: to play pool or billiards
I love to shoot pool with my friends after class.

shopping: *We should go grocery shopping soon because our refrigerator is almost empty!*

singing: *I really love singing, but other people don't enjoy my singing as much as I do.*

soccer: *Soccer is getting more popular in the United States, but it's still not a very popular sport there.*

sports: *Playing sports is a great way to keep fit and learn about teamwork.*

surfing the Internet: *I spent three hours surfing the Internet, but I still couldn't find the information I needed.*

swimming: *Kevin's shoulders are sore because he went swimming all afternoon.*

tennis: *Since the city put up the new lights by the court, we can play tennis after dark.*

yoga: *My wife and I take yoga classes three times a week.*

Pilates: *I took a yoga class last year, but this year I want to try Pilates.*

coins: *My relatives always keep the change from their overseas trips to give to me for my coin collection.*

dolls: *The little girl loves to gather all the dolls in her collection together for a tea party.*

stamps: *I keep all the stamps from envelopes sent from other countries so I can add them to my collection.*

3 UNIVERSITY

PERSONALITY OPPOSITES

brainiac: a very intelligent person; a person who always studies and gets good grades; can sometimes be used in a negative way
Mark is such a brainiac. He has a perfect TOEIC score and a high GPA.
I wish I was a brainiac like my brother. I have to struggle just to get decent grades.

slow learner: someone who struggles to learn things and might be seen as less intelligent compared to others. It is a negative term.
My elementary school teacher said that I was a slow learner because I couldn't read as well as others. But these days I read two books every month. I proved her wrong.

easy grader: a teacher that gives very generous and high scores
Mr. Crayne is such an easy grader. If you show up, you'll get an A.
I don't care about learning yoga. I'm just taking yoga class because the teacher is an easy grader.

hard grader: a teacher that is very stingy with high scores and often gives grades that are lower than students expect
My friend said not to take English Writing. The professor is a hard grader and gives too much homework.
Prof. Jones is a hard grader. I handed in a masterpiece and he gave me a C+.

geek; nerd: negative terms for someone who often is very interested in studying and often lacks social skills
Bill is such a geek. He's spends every weekend playing computer games. He never meets anyone.
I spent my first semester in the library, by myself. I think this is why people think I'm a nerd.

jock: a negative term about someone who is good at sports but is seen as unintelligent
Johnny is such a jock. He's great at basketball, but he can't even do basic math problems.
Many people think football players are jocks, but many are very intelligent.

idea person: a creative person who is good at coming up with ideas and solving problems
My group leader is an idea person. She's great at coming up with ideas for our projects.

detail person: someone who is very concerned about every detail. They like everything to be perfect. They are often the opposite of idea people, who are more concerned about the big picture.
James is such a detail person. Everything must be perfect before he submits his papers.

joiner: a person who joins many clubs and likes to belong to groups; a people person
I wasn't a joiner until I went to college. Now I belong to three clubs.
My younger sister is shy, but my older brother's a joiner.

loner: someone who likes, or does not mind, being alone. Very shy people are often loners.
My daughter was a loner in high school. I hope she makes some friends in college.
I've always been kind of a loner. Give me a good book and a soft sofa and I am happy.

lenient (good cop): permissive, easygoing. In movies and TV, policemen and detectives usually have partners, and one partner is usually strict, mean, or violent and the other is non-violent, sympathetic and helpful. Usually the good cop-bad cop routine is done when questioning someone about a crime. The good cop will be kind and try to gain the trust of the suspect and the bad cop will try to scare the person into talking. This routine is very common in interrogation scenes of TV shows like *NCIS* or *Law and Order*. In the *Lego* movie, Liam Neeson's cop character played both the good cop and the bad cop by turning his head around. Often, the cops are just pretending, so that they can scare somebody into cooperating. (Parents might do this also.) Instead of saying: *My father is strict and my mother is lenient,* you could say: *My mom is the good cop and my dad is the bad cop. Do your parents play "good cop-bad cop" when you come home late?*

strict (bad cop): harsh, severe. Professors sometimes have to be both good cop and bad cop (at different times, of course). A teacher might be a bad cop (to fuss at a class after they do poorly on a test) and a good cop (to encourage them). A teacher can also play "good cop-bad cop" all in one scene!
"You are late. You get an F!" "Oh, professor, please!" "Well, OK. You can take a makeup test tomorrow."
Is your father the good cop or the bad cop?

long attention span; short attention span: If you have a long attention span, you can study or concentrate for a long time (three to four hours). If you have a short attention span, you can only study, or concentrate, for a short time (twenty to thirty minutes). Generally, children (especially boys) have short attention spans. They ask things like: *"Are we there yet?"*
Do you have a long attention span? I had a long attention span in high school, but these days I need to take a break every half hour and take a nap every two hours.
I have a short attention span. I can never study more than one hour without taking a break. If I have coffee, I can go a little longer.

party animal: a person who likes to stay out late and party
Bill was a party animal right after he got out of the army.
Wow! Jack is a party animal, but he is so shy at work.
Those engineering majors are a bunch of party animals. They study hard and stay out really late.

party pooper: someone who wants to go home early from the party; someone who does not want to party. Pooped is slang for tired, exhausted.
It's only 10 o'clock! Don't be such a party pooper.
My date was a party pooper. Just when things were getting started, she wanted me to bring her home.

weekend warrior: a person who drinks a lot, but only on the weekends; they behave during the week, but on the weekends they let loose, relieve the stress, and party hardy

social drinker: someone who rarely drinks, usually only on social occasions, such as weddings; when Koreans say *Do you like to drink? Not really, I'm more of a social drinker. When my friends drink I usually just have one beer and sip it all night.*
My sister is a social drinker. She drinks every now and then, but never very much. Usually only at weddings.

teetotaler: someone who never drinks
My mother is a teetotaler. She never drank in her whole life.
"How was your date?" "Kind of a waste of money. The party had free booze, but she was a teetotaler."

studious; bookworm: someone who really enjoys studying and reading. "Studious" is a positive word, while "bookworm" is sometimes negative.
Jane is so studious. She is always in the library reading or working on homework.
Don't be such a bookworm, go outside and do something. You always have your nose in a book.

slacker: a person who hates and avoids studying or doing work
My father says that I'm a slacker. He says that I spend all day watching TV.
Many freshmen students are slackers. After years of being bookworms, they stop doing homework.

underachiever, overachiever: An overachiever is a smart person who performs below their abilities or potential. If you are very smart, but you make only C's, you are an underachiever. An overachiever underachiever. An overachiever is the opposite, and is someone who is not the smartest or best in class, but they try so hard that they have the best grade in class
Look at this. He has the highest IQ in class, and the lowest grades. What an under achiever. Time to talk to his parents.
I'm tired of you being an underachiever. Study or else.
I am worried that my son is an underachiever. He graduated from Seoul National University, but he's a taxi driver. I hope it's just a phase he's going through.
Sometimes overachievers try too hard and they end up quitting and dropping out.

alumni, alumnus: someone who graduated from a certain university; plural=*alumni*, singular= *alumnus*
The statue was donated by the alumni.

apply: to officially request permission to attend a school
How many schools did you apply to?

application: the official paperwork (letters and forms) that needs to be submitted to ask permission to attend a school
My application for Berkeley arrived in the mail today. I'm going to fill it out right now.

apply yourself: to try to do your best at something; to work hard
If you apply yourself this semester, you might be able to get a scholarship.

cafeteria: the big school restaurant for students
Do you want to eat in the school cafeteria or off campus?

cheat sheet: notes written on a small piece of paper, a hand, or an arm, for the purpose of cheating on an exam; a study guide
I made this cheat sheet for chemistry, but I was so worried that the professor would catch me that I didn't use it.

clique: a group of people with similar interests who do not interact much with people from outside the group
I don't like this school because there are too many cliques. Nobody will talk to me.

college; university; school: In countries other than America, a college is a two-year educational institution for students who have graduated high school. In America, a college and a university are the same thing. A university is a four-year educational institution for high school graduates; a school is any educational institution.
My sister couldn't get into a university after high school, so she went to college first. After college, she went to a university.

course; class; subject: a series of lessons on a given topic that count as credit towards a student's degree
I'm going to take summer courses this year, so I can graduate sooner.

cram: to push a large amount of material into a small amount of space; to study a lot of information in a short amount of time before an exam
It's my habit to cram for exams. So far, I've been successful at it.

credits: classes or courses taken by a student toward earning a degree
Oh no! I just realized that after this semester, I'm going to be just one credit short of my degree. I'll have to come back next year just for one credit.

hours: the number of hours spent in a class per week
This semester, I am taking 20 hours.

curriculum: the courses offered in a major; a plan including the material to be covered in a course, and the times at which it will be covered
I think the curriculum for archaeology majors looks very interesting.

dean: the head of a department; the person who takes care of the administration and business side of a department in a university or college
I talked to the dean of the chemistry department today. She's actually a very nice lady.

degree: the diploma or certificate students earns when they graduate
Many students put too much emphasis on getting their degree and not enough emphasis on learning.

double major: two major areas of study instead of one
She decided to do a double major to improve her chances of landing a good job after graduation.

drop-add period: a one- or two-week period at the beginning of a semester during which students can drop or add classes to their schedules
The drop-add period is only two weeks, so you must decide quickly if you like your classes or not.

exchange student: a student who studies in a foreign country as part of an agreement between schools
I really like my major, because it allows me to go to Spain as an exchange student.

excused absence: a class missed for a legitimate, forgivable reason, such as illness or a class trip
I had an excused absence last week because my grandfather died.

fail: to not pass a class
If I don't get at least a C+ on the final, I will fail this class.

flunk: to get a failing grade for an exam or course
I heard that this class is so easy. My friend said that it is impossible to flunk this class.

gap year: a year taken off before or during college, to study for entrance exams, travel, work, etc.
I plan to take a gap year before I start college to travel around Europe.

grade(s): a score earned on a test or for a class
What grade did you get in English class last semester?

medical excuse: an illness-related reason for missing a class
I had a medical excuse for missing class last week. I broke my leg in a car accident.

midterms, midterm exams: tests taken halfway through the semester
I have five classes this semester, but I only have three midterms.

post the grades: to make grades public; to show the grades for a class for students to see
We've been waiting for two weeks for the professor to post the grades for the final exam. He'd better hurry up.

procrastinate: to delay doing something
I should do my report this weekend, but I'll probably procrastinate and start on it the day before it is due.

pull an all-nighter: to study or work all night
I have two big essays due tomorrow. It looks like I'll be pulling an all-nighter.

recharge my batteries: take a rest or relax in order to regain one's energy
Last semester was so hard. I'm going to need a week or two to recharge my batteries before I start looking for a job.

attendance sheet: the list that contains the names of all the students in a certain class
I don't understand why teachers still use attendance sheets. They are so old-fashioned.

register: to enroll, or sign up for, a class
Freshmen will be able to start registering for classes on July 15th.

scholarship: money or free tuition given to a student for academic or athletic achievements, or for financial need
If I can maintain my GPA next semester, I will get a scholarship.

semester break: the time off between semesters
I can't believe it. My semester break is almost over.

skip class; play hooky: to miss class for no good reason
I'm really tired. I think I'll skip my morning classes today.

syllabus: the plan for a course of study, including the required textbooks and what will be covered week-by-week
The syllabus says that our midterm is on the 19th.

transfer: change from one school to another before graduating
Did you hear about Stella? She's going to transfer to UCLA.

tuition: the money paid to attend a school
I have to work this summer so I can pay tuition for next year.

apartment: a place where a student can rent a room (and maybe bathroom) and share a kitchen with other renters for a small amount of money
Do you know of any cheap apartments near the university?

commute: to travel a far distance to and from school or work each day
It takes me over an hour to commute to school in the morning.

dormitory, dorm: a building on campus for students to live in
I think I want to stay in a dorm next year.

off campus: not on the actual school grounds
There are a lot of apartments and bars off campus.

walking distance: a distance close enough to easily walk
There're a subway and a bus stop within walking distance of my home.

major: the main field of study chosen by a student
My parents want my major to be economics, but I want to study music.

minor: the secondary field of study chosen by a student
I chose Asian studies as a minor because I hope to work in Asia someday.

required course: a class that is mandatory in order to graduate
Unfortunately, Math 201 is a required course. I hate math!

elective course: a class that is not mandatory; an optional class
I think I'm going to take a psychology course for my elective next term.

4 SHOPPING

accessories: items such as purses, handbags, belts, earrings, and watches, that enhance the appearance of people and the clothes they wear
My wife always thinks about which accessories match her clothes, but I just wear my watch and don't think about it.

all the bells and whistles: having a lot of extra options, like a cell phone with an MP3 player, Internet access, and games
My new stereo has all the bells and whistles—wireless speakers, DVD player, and recorder.

baggy: loose-fitting
Most hip-hop stars and their fans wear baggy clothes these days.

bargain: something for sale at a price that is lower than normal
These shoes were such a bargain that I decided to buy two pairs.

bargain shopper: a person who only goes shopping when there are bargains or sales
My grandmother was a real bargain shopper. She would spend all day driving around town for the best prices.

big / small selection: a large number of items to choose from; a department store has a big selection, but a convenience store has a small selection
I like shopping here because they have a big selection of products.

brand-name; name brand: a product made by a famous company such as Samsung or Calvin Klein
My husband only buys brand-name electronics. Last year, he spent a lot of money on a Sony TV.

brand-new: very new
Your shoes are so white; they must be brand-new.

browse: to shop without the intention of buying; to just look; Koreans call this "eye shopping"
"Can I help you?" "No thanks, I'm just browsing." Let's go browse through the mall.

cashier: the person a customer pays money to in a store
You can take these jeans to the cashier to pay for them.

champagne taste: preference for things that cost a lot of money
"Why do you look so down, John?" "Oh, my wife has champagne taste, but we're living on a beer budget."

cheap (person): too careful about how one spends money (Note: This is an insulting term.)
My husband is so cheap that he buys all our birthday presents at the convenience store.

cheap merchandise: goods of low quality or at low prices
Let's not go to that shop. They only sell cheap merchandise.

cheap price: a low price
Wow! That's a really cheap price for notebook. Let's buy one.

convenience store: a store that is nearby and open long hours to be convenient for shopping
Could you stop by the convenience store and buy some milk? We're all out.

customer service: help and information given to customers in a store by the store's employees
If you have any problems with a product, just take it to the customer service desk and someone will help you.

defective: not working normally; flawed or broken
I think this calculator is defective. It won't multiply numbers. It just adds them.

designer label: an expensive product from a famous company
They cost more, but I only wear designer-label clothes.

dressing room; fitting room: a small room in which to try on clothes in a clothes shop
Why don't you try these on in the dressing room?

expensive: costing a lot of money
After I get my first paycheck, I'm going to buy an expensive watch.

fancy: very nice or of high quality
Wow. Nice fancy new clothes. Did you get a raise?

floor model: merchandise on display that is sometimes sold at a discount after all stock has been sold
I'm sorry, we only have this floor model left. I can give you 20% off if you want to buy it.

frugal; thrifty: very careful about how one spends money
My mother is frugal. She makes her own kimchi instead of buying it.

generic: common, low-cost merchandise; not a brand-name item
I always wear boots, so I just buy generic socks.

gyp, gypped: a bad bargain; cheated on the price of an item
This place is a gyp. They advertised Nikes but sold Mikes.
I got gypped. The saleswoman said this was a diamond, but it's just glass.

haggle: to bargain or negotiate over the price
My grandmother always haggles over vegetables at the market.
I haggled the price of this watch down to $30 dollars!

impulse buyer; impulse shopper: someone who buys a product on impulse, without thinking about it for a long time
"Why did you buy that ugly hat?" "What can I say? I'm an impulse buyer."

instant gratification: immediate satisfaction; fun or happiness without waiting
People want instant gratification. They don't want to wait for things.

knock-off: an illegal copy of a brand-name product
"Wow! Is that bag a Dolce & Gabbana? How much did you pay for it?" "Actually, it was cheap. This is just a knock-off."

look all over town: go to many different shops in search of some product
We looked all over town and finally found it in a little shop in Insadong.

luxurious: very comfortable and expensive
Wow. That fur coat is very luxurious. Your boyfriend must love you very much.

mom-and-pop store: a small independently owned store, not owned by a chain
My parents are retired, but they run a mom-and-pop grocery store. Their customers like the personal touch they can't find in a supermarket chain.

novelty shop: a store that sells odd merchandise
Did you try a novelty shop? They might have some furry socks.

one-stop shopping: shopping for everything in one place, like in a department store
I like one-stop shopping more than driving all over town to get what I need.

perfume; cologne: liquid to make people smell nice. Women wear perfume, and men wear cologne.
What kind of perfume is that? It smells great.

plastic: slang for credit card
"Do you take plastic?" "Certainly."

receipt: a paper given to a customer that lists the items he or she bought and how much each item cost
Let me see the receipt. I think they overcharged us for the tomatoes.

refund: money paid back to a customer
I'd like to return this sweater and get a refund.

rip-off, ripped off: something overpriced or of cheap quality; to be ripped off means to be cheated while shopping
I was ripped off. I thought I bought a Louis Vuitton bag, but it was a Lewis Veeton bag. What a rip-off!

shopaholic: a person who loves to go shopping, almost like an addiction
My girlfriend is a shopaholic. She is always at the mall.

shop till you drop: an exaggeration that means to shop for a long time until you are exhausted
We had fun at the mall last Saturday. We shopped till we dropped!

shopping spree: a shopping trip on which you buy a lot of things and spend a lot of money in a short amount of time
If I won the lottery, I would go on a shopping spree. I would buy so many things.

souvenir shop: a shop in which people buy souvenirs (i. e., things to remind people of a place, such as postcards, T-shirts, and key chains)
All of these souvenir shops sell the same junk.

splurge: to spend a lot of money
I don't like it when my husband goes to the electronics store. He always splurges.

street vendor: a small merchant who sells merchandise on the street rather than in a store
There are a lot of street vendors in Dongdaemun.

tacky: cheap-looking and out of style
Did you see that tacky old sofa they bought at the pawn shop?

the old bait and switch: a selling strategy, or trick, in which customers are lured to a store with a promise of a low-priced item, but then the salesclerk tries to sell them a higher-priced item
"Look at that price. It's too low." "Yeah, it looks like they are doing the old bait and switch."

tightwad: a person who is too careful about how he or she spends money (Note: This is an insulting term.)
She's such a tightwad. She never tips waiters.

top-end: of the highest quality
Where do the prices start for your top-end models?

used: previously owned and used by someone else; secondhand
I don't have a lot of money, so I want to buy a used car.

variety, various: a wide selection (variety); many different (various)
That department store has a wide variety of merchandise. There are various colors to choose from.

vary, varies: to be different from store to store
The price varies, so it could be cheap in one place but expensive in another.

wardrobe: all the clothes owned and worn by a person
He had to buy a whole new wardrobe for his new office job.

warranty; guarantee: a promise to replace a product or refund money if the product has a problem within a certain time after it is bought
This computer has a 90-day warranty on the hardware.

window shopping: to go shopping on a sidewalk or in a mall, just looking in the stores through the window, and not going in
Last weekend, my friend and I went window shopping in Myeong-dong.

5 MOVIES

based on, based upon: indicates the source of the story of a movie (Movies are often based on novels or true events.)
Did you know that this movie is based on the life of Ernest Hemingway?

character actor: an actor who usually plays interesting or unusual parts rather than leading roles (Gene Hackman, Tommy Lee Jones, and Anthony Hopkins are character actors.)
Willem Dafoe is one of my favorite character actors. His movies are always so interesting.

chemistry: a positive, energetic feeling between two people or two things
Brad Pitt and Angelina Jolie had a lot of on-screen chemistry. And evidently a lot of off-screen chemistry, also.

chick flick / date flick: a chick flick is a movie that women would like; a date flick is a movie suitable for a date as it appeals to both men and women and has a happy mood
I don't want to see The Notebook. *It's a chick flick. Let's go see* World War Z.

cut to the chase: an expression meaning "hurry up" or "get to the point" that is derived from movie language. If a movie scene is too long and boring, the director might decide to cut part of the scene to get directly to the car chase, which is a

more exciting part of the movie.
I don't have time to listen to all your excuses. Just cut to the chase and tell where your homework is.

director: the artist who makes the movie
I really want to see the movie Jazz English 3. *The director always makes amazing films.*

producer: the person who funds a movie
If I had a lot of money, I would love to be a movie producer.

ensemble cast: a group of several famous actors in a movie in which no one actor has the lead role. For example, the Korean movie *Thieves* has an ensemble cast.
I thought the ensemble cast in Ocean's 11 *did a wonderful job.*

far-fetched: hard to believe; unbelievable
Those scenes in outer space in Armageddon *were kind of far-fetched.*

femme fatale: a sexy but dangerous female character
Kim Hye-soo always plays the femme fatale. She was especially good in Ta Cha.

flashback: part of a movie in which the action moves from the present time to a time in the past
The movie had too many flashbacks. I got confused.

genre: the type or style of movie; for example, action-adventure or comedy
I think romantic comedies are the best genre to see on a date.

girl-next-door type: a woman or girl whose style is fairly normal rather than flashy
"Han Ga-in often plays the girl-next-door type." "Yeah, I wish the girl next door to me looked like her!"

gory: showing extreme amounts of blood and violence
I didn't like all the blood and guts in that movie, Saw. *It was too gory for me.*

happy ending: when the climax and final scenes of a movie leave the viewers feeling happy about the story
My little sister likes movies with happy endings, like Frozen.

hard to follow: a plot with many twists, flashbacks, or other confusing features that make it difficult for viewers to always understand what is happening
A lot of people didn't like Pulp Fiction *because the plot was hard to follow.*

leading man / leading lady: the actors who play the main male and female characters in a movie
Who played the leading man?

macho; tough guy: a strong man who beats up bad guys and feels no pain
Stop trying to act macho. I know that hurts.

parody; satire: something that makes fun of a serious topic
The Austin Powers movies are parodies of James Bond movies.

platonic relationship: a relationship that involves friendship rather than romance or sex
I think it's really difficult for a man and woman to have a close, platonic relationship.

plot: the story and actions in a movie
That movie's plot was too complicated. I was lost before the first explosion.

theme: the message or main idea of a movie
The theme of Guardians of the Galaxy *is that the good guys always win.*

plot twist: when an action or scene in a movie is surprising or unexpected
LA Confidential *was very interesting because it had a lot of plot twists.*

predictable: when a plot provides no mystery, suspense, or tension; when viewers know what will happen before it happens in the movie
That movie was too predictable. I have seen that plot a dozen times before.

remake: a movie that is a modern version of an older movie
"That movie was a remake." "Really? Who was in the original?"

sappy: too sentimental; when a movie relies on clichés to express love and sadness too strongly
The scene in Titanic *when DiCaprio was in the water freezing and told the girl not to worry was too sappy.*

sequel: a second, third, or even fourth movie that is a continuation of the story from an original movie, such as the Batman series
I find that the sequel is not usually as good as the original.

snooty rich type: a character that believes he or she is better than others because of money—for example,
Kate Winslet's fiancé in Titanic *was the snooty rich type. Everyone was hoping he would drown.*

sold out: a movie or event to which all the tickets have already been sold
I wanted to go see the latest Star Wars *movie on the first night, but it was sold out.*

special effects: scenes or additions to scenes that are created by models, computers, or special filming techniques rather than just actors
The recent James Bond movies rely too much on special effects and not enough on a good story.

supporting actor: an actor who plays a character who is of secondary importance to the lead character
Morgan Freeman is my favorite supporting actor. He was great in Million Dollar Baby.

surprise ending: when the climax and resolution of the main problem of the plot are very unexpected
My favorite surprise ending to a movie was probably in The Usual Suspects.

the bad guy; villain: the main character that causes problems for the hero or leading man or woman in a movie
I think the best villain of all time is Darth Vader from Star Wars.

BASIC MOVIE TYPES & PLOTS

amnesia film: a movie in which the leading character forgets his or her past
The Bourne Identity *is an example of an amnesia film. Matt Damon's character has to figure out why people are trying to kill him, but he can't remember who he is.*

black comedy: a comedy about a serious or tragic subject
American Beauty *is one of my favorite black comedies.*

boy meets girl, boy loses girl, boy gets girl: a common plot in movies and TV shows, in which the male and female characters meet, are forced apart by some events, then they overcome the problems and live happily ever after
It was a typical boy-meets-girl, boy-loses-girl, boy-gets-girl story. No suspense.

buddy film: a movie in which the two main characters are close friends (buddies) who go through adventures together
The Shawshank Redemption *and* Rush Hour *are two examples of buddy films.*

Cinderella plot: a story line in which a poor pretty girls' life becomes wonderful because a rich man falls in love with her
Love in Paris *was a Korean TV show with a Cinderella plot.*

coming-of-age film: a movie in which children or teenagers learn important life lessons and become adults
Mona Lisa Smile *and* Dead Poets Society *are two of my favorite coming-of-age films. Both are very sad.*

dialog-driven film: a movie that relies mostly on the conversations of its characters rather than actions
I don't usually like dialogue-driven movies, but I did enjoy Before Sunrise.

historical drama: a serious movie about some historical subject
Historical dramas are some of my favorite movies. I love being taken back into time, like in Gone With the Wind, Gladiator *and* The Patriot.

horror movie: a very scary, violent movie, such as *Friday the 13th* and *I Know What You Did Last Summer*
I like horror movies that are scary rather than gory, so I liked A Tale of Two Sisters *more than* Saw.

love triangle: a movie that features a man in love with two women or a woman in love with two men
Love triangles can make for an interesting plot, like in Gone With the Wind. *I really liked that movie.*

prison film: a movie that takes place in a prison or jail
I think people like prison films because we all feel trapped in some way. Movies like The Green Mile *and* The Shawshank Redemption *show that good people are sometimes put in prison.*

puppy love: a movie in which the main characters are young and feel intense, but not long-lasting love
I hate movies about puppy love. They remind me too much of when I was young.

revenge movie: a movie about people doing harm to those who did them harm; for example, *Old Boy*
The movie I saw last weekend was OK. It was a typical revenge movie.

road film: a movie in which the main characters travel, usually by car
I love the adventure shown in road movies. Due Date *is one of my favorite road movies.*

science fiction: highly imaginative fiction that usually involves technical or futuristic plots
I like science fiction movies that have interesting stories, like Star Wars *and* The Matrix.

slapstick comedy: a funny movie in which the humor is derived from the actions (such as falling, sliding, hitting) of the characters rather than from their words
Jim Carrey is really funny in slapstick comedies. Dumb and Dumber *is hilarious.*

slasher film: a type of horror film in which the villain kills many other characters by cutting (slashing) them with a large knife, sword, or chain saw
I used to like slasher films, like Friday the 13th *and* Halloween, *but now I find them boring.*

tearjerker: a movie that tries very hard to make the viewers cry
I don't usually like tearjerkers, but Philadelphia *made me feel quite sad, and I liked it.*

unrequited love: a story in which one character loves another, but that love is not returned
The Phantom of the Opera *is a good example of a movie about unrequited love.*

Western; cowboy movie: a film set in the American West during the late 1800s
My father really loves Westerns. He loves the tough cowboy that always stands for justice.

6 FOOD & RESTAURANTS

all-you-can-eat: used to describe a restaurant (or special offer) in which customers can eat as much as they want for one price
Every Monday, I go to the all-you-can-eat pizza buffet. It's a great way to eat a lot for not much money.

atmosphere; mood: the surroundings, interior decoration, music, and attitude of the servers of a restaurant, coffee shop, or pub
I really enjoy the relaxing atmosphere of this Italian restaurant.

brown bag lunch: lunch brought to school or work from home, rather than bought at a restaurant (Traditionally, many Americans brought it in a brown paper bag.)
I'd like to go to the restaurant with you, but I brought a brown bag lunch today.

brunch: a combination of the words "breakfast" and "lunch," referring to a meal usually eaten between 9 a.m. and 12 p.m.
My family goes out for Sunday brunch every weekend after church.

chocoholic: a person who is addicted to chocolate (The suffix "-holic" means "addicted to.")
My wife always buys chocolate; she's a chocoholic.

complimentary; on the house: free; given without charge by a restaurant or shop
I really like Italian restaurants because they serve delicious complimentary bread.

delicious: tastes really good
The food at our cafeteria is delicious. Well, maybe not delicious, but pretty good.

diet: the food one eats; a plan to lose weight
The doctor said I'm not getting enough vegetables in my diet.

drive-through (drive-thru): a fast-food restaurant at which a customer can order, pay for, and receive his or her food without leaving a car
Let's just use the drive-through. I want to get home before the hockey game starts.

eat-in or take-out?: a question commonly asked by cashiers at fast-food restaurants; eat-in indicates staying in the restaurant to eat, and take-out indicates taking the food away from the restaurant to eat
"Is that order to eat in or take out?" "Hmm, I think we'll stay here, so eat in, please."

ethnic food: food from another culture that is not very common in your country (For example, Indian food would be considered ethnic food in Korea, but Japanese or Italian food would not.)
"Let's go try that new Egyptian restaurant." "No, thanks. I don't feel like ethnic food."

fancy food: special, expensive food that is not easily prepared
Jim doesn't like fancy food. He prefers something simple, like hamburgers.

fast food: food that does not take a long time to prepare, like hamburgers and fried chicken
Fewer people are eating fast food these days because it's not very healthy.

food poisoning: a severe stomach/intestinal illness resulting from eating spoiled food, such as raw beef or seafood containing harmful bacteria
He had to go to the hospital after he ate that sushi and got food poisoning last July.

foodie; gourmet; connoisseur: a lover of good or fancy food; someone with a taste for fancy, expensive food or other products, such as an art connoisseur; a foodie is someone who really loves food
Jack always knows the best restaurants. He's a foodie. My cousin studied cooking in Paris. Now she's a real gourmet.

free refills: a service offered by some restaurants to refill a cup of cola, tea, or coffee at no extra charge
You can drink as much cola as you like. They have free refills here.

freebie: something given for free, such as a free sample from a department store or a supermarket
"Where did you get that pizza?" "It was a freebie from that restaurant that just opened."

high-calorie: containing a large amount of fat and calories
Doughnuts are a really high-calorie food.

low-calorie: containing a small amount of fat and low caloric count
Fruits and vegetables are good low-calorie food choices.

high-cholesterol: containing a large amount of cholesterol (unhealthy fat from animals)
That fried chicken is high-cholesterol. You shouldn't eat it.

low-cholesterol: containing a small amount of cholesterol
This is a special, low-cholesterol chicken burger, so it's healthy to eat.

junk food: unhealthy food; includes fast food as well as snacks such as potato chips, chocolate, ice cream, and doughnuts
I know I shouldn't, but I eat junk food as a snack every afternoon.

leftovers: food that remains (is left over) after a meal and then reserved for a future meal
We always eat a lot of leftovers during the week after Chusok.

messy eater: a person who spills food all over his or her clothes and the table while eating
If you get food or sauce all over your shirt or tie or pants while you are eating, you are a messy eater.

mouth-watering: describes a food that looks or smells so good that it makes people's mouths water in hunger
She always cooks the most mouth-watering meals. I can't wait for dinner!

It's my treat. / It's on me: expressions to indicate "I will pay for it."
Don't worry about it. Lunch is my treat.

nibble: to eat a small amount; to take a small bite
Sometimes, when she's not really hungry, she will just nibble on an apple for lunch.

nutritious: healthy; filled with vitamins and nutrients
Fruit makes a much more nutritious snack than chocolate.

pick up the tab: to pay for something, such as a meal in a restaurant
The good thing about working there is that the boss picks up the tab for lunch every day.

picky eater: a person who is very selective in what he or she eats
It's always difficult to take my son to a restaurant because he's such a picky eater. He doesn't like anything.

pig out: to eat a lot till one is completely full
When I was a kid, my friends and I used to totally pig out on hot dogs. I could eat six or seven without getting sick.

ritzy / fancy restaurant: a fancy and expensive restaurant, like one at the Ritz Hotel
Wow. This restaurant is quite ritzy. I hope you brought a lot of money.

salt and pepper: two common seasonings that add flavor to food, often placed together on a table
These potatoes are bland. Could you pass me the salt and pepper, please?

sip: to take a small drink of (similar to *nibble* for eating)
Be careful! That coffee is very hot. Just sip it a little.

guzzle: to drink rapidly nonstop
I like to sip champagne, but I guzzle beer.

stuffed: very full; used to describe a stomach full of food
After Thanksgiving dinner, the whole family was stuffed.

sweet tooth: a fondness for sweet foods such as cake, candy, pie, doughnuts, etc.
My father has a sweet tooth.

theme restaurant: a restaurant with a special design and atmosphere (For example, a Disney theme restaurant would have many pictures, sculptures, and even menu items named after Disney characters.)
My kids always like to go to that Snoopy theme restaurant for their birthday parties.

throw up: to push food or drink out of the stomach and out of the mouth; other words and phrases with the same meaning: *vomit, barf, upchuck, toss your cookies, lose your lunch*
My friend drank too much soju last night and threw up on the street.

upset stomach: a feeling of stomach pain and/or nausea (feeling like you have to throw up)
Sometimes I get an upset stomach if I drink too much soju.

vegetarian: a person who does not eat meat
I'm a vegetarian, but if I have no choice, I'll eat meat.

RESTAURANT FOOD CATEGORIES

appetizer: a small or light food such as French bread and butter, a shrimp cocktail, or calamari (Italian-style fried squid rings) served before the main dish of a meal
Let's get some appetizers before dinner. I'm so hungry, I don't want to wait.

dessert: a sweet food served after the meal; in Western countries, this is typically cake, pie, fruit, or ice cream, though (In Western countries, this is typically cake, pie, fruit, or ice cream, though in Korea, it can be coffee or cola.)
That dessert menu looks great, but I'm already stuffed from dinner. Maybe next time.

main dish: entrée; the largest part of a meal, usually a meat or pasta dish
I'm not that hungry. I think I'll just get an appetizer instead of a main dish.

side dish; side order: food served in addition to (beside) the main dish
I'll have the roast chicken, please, and a side order of rice.

RESTAURANT PEOPLE

chef: a person with a lot of training who cooks food in a fancy restaurant
She went to Paris to study to become a chef. I can't wait until she comes back and cooks for us.

cook: a person with little training who cooks simple foods in a fast-food restaurant
I used to be a cook in a fast-food restaurant. I hated that job!

hostess / host: a person who greets customers at a restaurant and finds them an appropriate table
Please tell the hostess that we want a table for two in the no-smoking area.

waiter / waitress: a person who takes orders and serves food in a restaurant
You should give the waiter a $20 tip; he was so friendly and helpful.

TASTE

hot: spicy in taste; hot in temperature
Look how red that kimchi is. I'll bet it's really hot.

spicy: with a pleasantly strong, burning flavor
Please give me some more chili paste. I really like spicy food.

bland: with little or no taste or flavor ("Mild" describes foods that taste good because of flavors are weak, not spicy.)
This soup is really bland. I'm going to add some chili paste to it.

fresh: new or recently produced
I just bought some fresh corn at the supermarket.

stale: the opposite of fresh; picked or made long ago so that it has lost a lot of flavor
This bread is hard and stale. I don't want to eat it.

sweet: sugary-tasting
I love sweet things. I can't get enough cake and ice cream at a buffet.

sour: acidic-tasting like lemon or vinegar
I don't know why people love lemonade, it's too sour. I prefer the sweet taste of iced tea.

STEAK

raw: rare; cooked for a short time (Literally, this means completely uncooked but is used as an exaggeration when ordering steak.)
My uncle always orders his steak raw.

rare: cooked for a short time; very red on the inside
I like my steak cooked rare.

medium rare: dark on the outside and pink on the inside
My brother likes his steak medium rare.

medium: dark on the outside and a little pink in the middle
My mother usually orders her steak medium.

well done: no visible pink on the inside
My dad likes his steak well done, but I think it's way too tough to chew.

burnt: cooked for a long time so that the outside is black and crisp
My grandfather always orders his steak burnt. I don't know how he can eat it.

PIZZA

thin crust: the bread part of the pizza that that is thin and dry
I'd like a thin-crust pizza, please.

thick crust: the bread part of the pizza that that is thick and greasy
When I was young, I used to love thick-crust pizza.

deep-dish pan pizza: the bread part of the that pizza is very thick
When I was in university, my friends and I always ordered deep-dish pan pizza. It was delicious.

CHICKEN

white meat: light-colored meat, usually from the breast
My wife and I both like white meat, so we always leave the drumsticks when we eat chicken.

dark meat: dark-colored meat, usually from the leg and wing
When we eat chicken, my kids always fight over who gets to eat the dark meat, like the drumstick and wings.

crispy; crunchy: cooked so that the outer surface is a little hard and makes a sound when bitten
My mother used to make delicious crispy chicken. It was really crunchy, but not greasy.

greasy: cooked with or containing grease; oily
We ate a lot of greasy fried chicken tonight. Let's have some spicy kimchi now to cut through the oil.

fried: cooked in hot oil
You shouldn't eat too much fried food. It's not healthy.

grilled: cooked on a grill, over a flame
I prefer grilled chicken because it is healthier than fried.

baked: cooked in an oven for a long time
My mother baked a pie for Thanksgiving.

CHIPS & DIP

chips: many types of crunchy snacks such as potato chips and corn chips (In England, "chips" means French fries.)
Could you buy me a bag of chips at GS25? I've got the munchies.

dip: a thick sauce for dipping chips and snacks into to add more flavor
I really like to have this spicy dip with my corn chips.

7 SPORTS & EXERCISE

10K race: a ten-kilometer race
Are you running in the 10K race this weekend?

marathon: a 42.195-kilometer (26-mile) race
I used to be really fit. I ran several marathons.

amateur athlete: an athlete who does not get paid for performing in a sport
I really enjoy the Olympics because all the athletes are amateurs. They compete because they love the sport.

athletic: good at sports; physically talented
His mother is very athletic. She swims every day, and she won the city tennis tournament last year.

athletic scholarship: money for a student's school costs on the condition that the student play for one of the university's sports teams
She was a great volleyball player in high school, so she got an athletic scholarship to go to Yale.

awkward: not physically coordinated; poor at sports
He looks really awkward when he dribbles the basketball. He's not smooth at all.

beer belly: large stomach
I'm starting to get a beer belly. I think I should start working out.

calisthenics: exercises for warming up the muscles before playing a sport
When I served in the army, we did an hour of calisthenics every morning.

club membership: authority or ability to enter a group, or club, such as a health club or a golf club
I have a club membership for that gym through my company.

couch potato: a lazy person who sits on a sofa (couch) and watches TV all the time
My wife gets angry at me sometimes because I'm such a couch potato.

crash diet: a very strict, severe, sudden diet
I went on a crash diet two weeks before the wedding so I could fit into my dress, but I got very sick afterward.

endurance; stamina: the ability to exercise or work for a long time
I don't have enough endurance to run a marathon, so I'm going to try a half marathon instead.

exhausted: very tired
She's been working on that project all day. Now, she looks exhausted.

fit: healthy; in good physical condition
Two years ago, he was not in good shape, but since he began exercising, he looks very fit.

fitness freak; fitness fanatic: someone who is obsessed with exercise
My brother is a fitness freak. He exercises before and after work and sometimes even during his lunch hour.

flab, flabby: slang for "fat"
Drinking beer can make you flabby, so I drink soju instead.

graceful: the opposite of awkward; the ability to move one's body smoothly with coordination
That figure skater is so graceful.

gym: an indoor place where people can exercise and play sports such as basketball and volleyball
He works out in the gym every day after work.

hard-core: believing very strongly in something or doing something very intensely
She's a hard-core golfer. She goes to the driving range every morning.

health club; fitness club; health center; fitness center: a place where members pay money each month to use exercise facilities
I wanted to join that health club, but it was too expensive. Instead, I work out at the YMCA.

in shape, get in shape, out of shape, in good shape: refers to the physical condition of someone's body. "In shape" and "in good shape" refer to a fit body, and "out of shape" refers to an unfit body.
She is in very good shape. She can run a marathon in about three hours.

jock: someone who is athletic and good at sports
A lot of people stereotype jocks as stupid, but many athletes are very intelligent.

killer abs: well-defined or ripped stomach muscles; a six-pack
I'm going to keep doing sprints and crunches until I have killer abs.

last one picked: the person chosen last for a team (This means the person is not athletic.)
I hate playing team sports in PE class. I'm always the last one picked.

muscular: having large muscles
After lifting weights for a year, my brother has become quite muscular.

natural athlete: a person who is good at sports without much practice
She's good at tennis, golf, baseball, basketball. She's a real natural athlete.

No pain, no gain: nothing can be accomplished without effort
Your muscles won't get bigger if you only work out for ten minutes a week. No pain, no gain.

pace: the rate, speed per time, of something
You must walk at a faster pace to exercise your heart.

pace yourself: to control one's rate of exercise so as not to get tired too soon
You're running too fast. If you want to finish this marathon, you'll have to pace yourself.

panting: breathing heavily
The whole class was panting after that aerobics class.

PE; Phys. Ed.; physical education: an exercise class for students
My favorite part of PE was when we played dodgeball.

PE uniform: special clothes worn by students in exercise class
Our PE uniforms are in our school colors—red and black.

pooped: very tired, exhausted
I'm pooped. Let's take a break.

professional athlete; pro: an athlete who is paid to play a sport
His dream is to become a professional athlete someday. He really wants to be a pro hockey player.

pull a muscle: to suddenly stretch a muscle too far, causing pain and damage to the muscle
She pulled a muscle in her leg when she ran the 50-meter sprint. Now she has to relax for two weeks.

referee: someone who takes part in a sporting event to make sure the players follow the rules and get punished for breaking the rules
That referee always blows his whistle and calls too many penalties.

sprint: a short, fast race; to run in a short fast race
Run ten sprints across the gym and then hit the showers.

stretch: to make longer or wider; to gently pull muscles before exercising
We do a lot of stretching in my yoga class.

sweat: to excrete water and salt from one's skin during exercise or heat; the water and salt excreted from one's skin
I always need a nice long shower after jogging because I sweat so much.

track and field: sporting events that happen on a running track or on a field inside the track, like the decathlon and pentathlon events at the Olympics
I enjoy watching the track and field events at the Olympics.

warm up: to stretch and do light exercises before playing a sport or doing difficult exercises
We always warm up for about ten minutes before we play soccer.

work out, workout: to exercise (*work out*); the time spent and movements done during exercise (*workout*)
I usually work out for three hours a week. My workouts usually last one hour each.

yoga: a form of stretching and meditation
My wife and I take yoga classes three times a week.

Pilates: an exercise system similar to yoga that stresses building muscle strength while stretching
I took a yoga class last year, but this year I want to try Pilates.

cheerleader: someone who supports a team by leading cheers and dances
Amy is head cheerleader and the most popular girl in school. She'll never go out with me.

coach: the person who trains athletes or is in charge of a team
I quit the team because the coach was a real jerk. He only played the players he liked.

umpire: someone who takes part in a sporting event to make sure the players follow the rules and get punished for breaking the rules
That umpire calls to many strikes. He makes it really hard on the batters.

Note: Some sports have referees. Some have umpires.

ache: dull, constant pain; to feel a dull, constant pain
I played tennis for three hours today. Now my shoulder aches.

sore: to feel slight, constant pain
My legs are sore after skating yesterday afternoon.

muscle cramp: sudden tightening of a muscle that causes pain
He pulled out of the race because he had a muscle cramp.

blister: a skin bubble developed from too much rubbing
I have blisters on my feet after running in that marathon.

sprain: to damage the tissue around a joint, like an ankle or knee, so that pain and swelling occur
I can't walk for a week because I sprained my ankle playing basketball last weekend.

8 VACATIONS & TRAVEL

3-day weekend: when a holiday falls on a Friday or Monday, people have a 3-day weekend
Yes! July 4th is on a Monday this year, so we get a 3-day weekend.

4-day, 3-night: a trip package in which 4 days and 3 nights are spent away from home
We got a 4-day, 3-night package trip to Jeju Island for this Christmas.

airsick / carsick / seasick: feeling like you have to throw up because of too much movement
I never get airsick or seasick, but sometimes I get carsick during long drives.

backpacking: hiking through the countryside or wilderness while carrying equipment and food in a backpack
Every summer, my dad and I go on a backpacking trip through the mountains.

bags / suitcases / luggage: what you carry your clothes in for travel
How many bags did you pack for the trip? I'm taking three suitcases. That is way too much luggage.

bed and breakfast: a privately owned house in which the owners rent out some of their bedrooms and provide breakfast for their guests
I like to stay in a bed and breakfast because the owners can usually teach me a lot about the area.

bumper-to-bumper: of or relating to very crowded, slow-moving traffic
Driving to Busan on a holiday always takes forever because the traffic is bumper-to-bumper for hundreds of kilometers.

check in / check out: to officially arrive at or leave a hotel; the desk or area in which hotel guests officially arrive or leave
This receipt says we have to check out by noon tomorrow.

check it out: expression meaning "look at it" or "experience it"
I've heard this movie is really interesting. Do you want to go check it out?

crystal-clear: extremely clear and easy to see through or understand
The sea in the Caribbean is crystal clear. You can see everything on the sea floor.

ETA (estimated time of arrival): refers to the time at which someone or something is expected to arrive
What is your ETA? I should be there at about 7 o'clock.

folk village: a place that shows traditional houses and ways of life from the past
Our trip to the folk village was so interesting. I like learning about history.

frequent-flyer miles: credit given by airlines for each mile a customer has flown
I have finally saved enough frequent-flyer miles to take my family to Guam this winter.

hassle: a complication or an annoyance or something difficult to resolve; to bother someone
Getting our visas to visit China was a real hassle. My mother keeps hassling me to clean my room.

hiking / climbing: walking outdoors in the country or wilderness (hiking); using ropes to go up the side of a mountain or cliff (climbing)
I like to go hiking in the mountains around my home. Someday, I'd really like to try climbing up a rock cliff, too.

homestay: staying at the home of a family, instead of at a hotel
I'm afraid to do a homestay because in that country the host families are not supervised by the government.
When I went to Canada, I stayed at a homestay. The family was really nice.

jet lag: a temporary disruption of bodily rhythms after traveling a long distance across several time zones
I always get such bad jet lag when I fly to Europe.

layover: time spent in an airport between connecting flights
I have a two-hour layover in Seattle before I continue to New York.

lost: not knowing where one is; no longer in the possession of something
We tried to find the pyramids in the jungle, but we kept getting lost. My husband's passport is lost. We can't find it.

one-way / round-trip / open-return: different types of passage tickets for planes, buses, ships, or trains; one-way is only toward a destination; round-trip is to the destination and back to the original location; open-return means the traveler can choose any time to come back to the original location
I'd like a one-way ticket to Chicago, please.
Are there any open-return tickets available to Singapore? I'm not sure how long I want to stay.

overnight: lasting for one night
This weekend, I'm going to visit my grandmother in Daejeon. We're going to stay there overnight and come back in the morning.

package tour: a trip that a group of people take together that usually includes hotel, airfare, meals, and a guided tour
I didn't like that package tour. There was too much hurrying around from place to place.

pamper, pampered: to treat very kindly and take care of all needs in a luxurious setting
I like to stay at the Ritz because they always pamper me.

passport: an official document that shows someone's citizenship and is needed to travel
I have to renew my passport. It will expire in six months.

peace and quiet: a relaxing, calm, quiet time and atmosphere
She needs a lot of peace and quiet to study well. We're going to spend our vacation at a beach resort to get some peace and quiet.

peak time; peak season: the time period when the most people travel to a certain location; this usually leads to price increases
I only have vacation during peak season. It is so hard to find cheap tickets.

pollution: dirty, unhealthy materials put into the air, water, or land
The air pollution in Seoul gets worse each year.

R&R (rest and relaxation): a short time away from work for rest and fun
It's been a stressful week. Let's go to the lake this weekend for a little R&R.

relax, relaxing / take a break: to spend time without working or using a lot of energy (relax); related to an activity or sound that helps remove stress (relaxing); to take a short time away from work to relax (take a break, but Note: NEVER say, write, or think "take a rest")
Let's take a break. We can go relax by the fountain outside. I find the sound of the water very relaxing.

reservation: an appointment made for a flight, hotel room, or rental car
We made reservations for the Hilton downtown.

rip-off: a price that is too high for an item; a place that charges too much money for what it sells
Thirty dollars for that T-shirt is a rip-off. That restaurant is a rip-off. They charge five dollars for a glass of cola.

room service: food or drinks delivered by the hotel staff to a guest's hotel room
I like the idea of room service, but I hate paying the high prices.

rough it: to stay in the wilderness without modern tools and conveniences
When we go hiking, we like roughing it. We sleep in a tent and cook all our food over a campfire.

scenic route: a road with a nice view
The scenic route takes 30 minutes longer to drive, but the scenery is much nicer.

scenic view: a beautiful view
Let's pull over and take some pictures of that scenic view. The mountains and lake are so pretty!

semester break: a time of no classes between semesters
How long is your semester break?

sightseeing: the act of visiting interesting sights of an area
Last weekend, we went sightseeing near Seoraksan.

souvenir: something bought as a reminder of a vacation or place
We bought this painting as a souvenir of our trip to Tahiti.

stressful: causing nervousness, anxiety, stress
I don't like to travel abroad. It's too stressful not knowing the language and customs.

tentative plans: hopeful, possible plans that might change
I have tentative plans to play tennis this weekend, but I may have to work.

tourist trap: a place that takes advantage of an area that tourists like to visit and charges very high prices
We just paid $20 for a sandwich and a cola. The view from here is nice, but what a tourist trap!

travel light: to bring very few clothes and other items when traveling
I am going to travel light for this trip. I'm just bringing one extra shirt and one extra pair of pants.

travel agency: a company that helps plan vacations and trips
I always used to use a travel agency, but now I plan my own vacations and buy tickets online.

trip / vacation: a trip involves travel to another area; a vacation is a time away from work or school, which can be spent staying at home or traveling
My wife and I took a trip to China last spring. During next summer vacation, I want to take a trip to Jejudo.

turbulence: an area of violent or uneven air-flow, causing a plane to shake
We had a rough flight. We experienced turbulence for most of the flight.

view: what can be seen from a hotel room or area, such as a mountain view, city view, ocean view, etc.
How was the view from your hotel? We had a nice view of the ocean sunsets.

visa: a document granting official permission to travel, study, work, or live in another country
My American friend got a visa to visit Korea for six months. My visa is only for one month.

youth hostel: cheap, often shared accommodations for young travelers
We will save lots of money by staying at youth hostels as we backpack across Europe.

Places to go

aquarium: a place for public viewing of aquatic plants and animals
I like to watch the sea turtles whenever I visit the aquarium.

historical district: an area where buildings and landmarks of historic or architectural significance are preserved
Walking through a historical district is like a going through time.

museum: a building in which works of scientific, artistic, or historical value are collected, cared for, and displayed
Seeing a Picasso painting in a book is one thing, but seeing one in a museum is much better.

theme park: an amusement park in which all of the components of the park are based on one or more themes
We felt like explorers while in the jungle area of the theme park.

zoo: a place for public viewing of animals
I could watch the monkeys at the zoo for hours.

Beach

jet skiing: the act of riding a motorized watercraft that can support one or two people who straddle the seat and steer the craft with handlebars
Jet skiing is a lot like riding a motorcycle on the water.

parasailing: the act of being pulled by a boat while harnessed to a parachute that enables one to fly over the water
I had a great view of the entire bay when I went parasailing.

sailing: the act of riding on a boat that is propelled through the water by wind, which is harnessed by large pieces of material attached to a vertical pole
Sailing is fun, but can be difficult if there isn't a strong wind.

scuba diving: the act of exploring underwater with the aid of a mask and oxygen tank to enable one to see and breathe while underwater
If you go scuba diving, you should take along an underwater camera.

snorkeling: the act of swimming with a mask and a plastic tube that aids in breathing
Snorkeling is a fun way to explore shallow waters.

sunbathing: the act of laying in the sun
She enjoys sunbathing for short periods of time, but she knows that too much can be harmful.

surfing: the act of riding waves while standing on a wooden or heavy plastic board
Hawaii is a great place for surfing.

swimming : the act of propelling oneself through the water with the use of one's limbs
The water was great. We went swimming at noon and swam for three hours.

waterskiing: the act of gliding over the water's surface by being pulled by a boat with two long, narrow pieces of wood or heavy plastic attached to one's feet
One needs great balance for waterskiing.

windsurfing: the act of riding over waves on a wooden or heavy plastic board with a sail attached to it
I love windsurfing because I can jump over the waves and do flips.

Snow

ski lift: the cable and seats that carry skiers up the mountain
I'm always nervous when I get off the ski lift. I always think that I'm going to fall or stay on too long.

ski pass: a ticket that allows a person to ski at a ski resort
I have to buy a ski pass for High One. It's my favorite place to ski.

snowboarding: the act of sliding down a hill on a snowboard, which is like a skateboard without wheels
Snowboarding is so much fun; it's much better than skiing.

Mountains
camping: sleeping outdoors, usually in a tent or in a camper
I just bought a brand new tent and sleeping bag. I can't wait to go camping this weekend.

white-water rafting: going down a fast moving river in an inflatable raft
My club is going white-water rafting this weekend. I'm so excited. I'm such an adrenaline junkie.

14 BOARD GAMES

BOARD GAME CONSTRUCTION

The next eight pages are two board games.
1. Cut them out of the book.
2. Tape them together so that they look like the ones below.
3. After you tape them, you will have two board games, back to back. Cool.
4. Take them to a copy shop or school supply and have them coated.
5. While there, buy some dice. (You can use a coin as a marker to move around the board.)

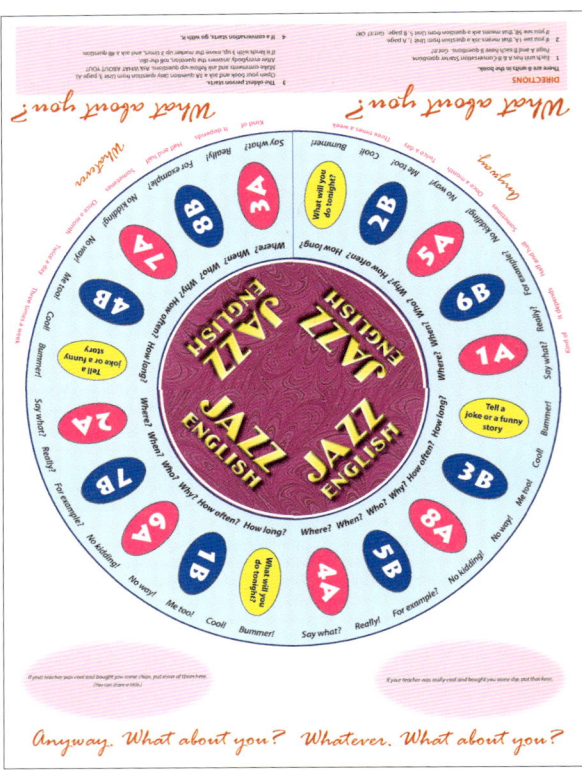

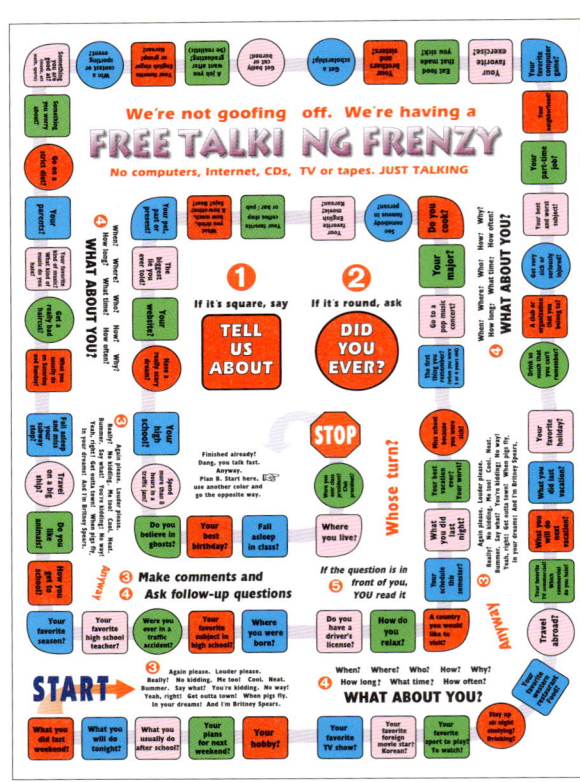

HOW TO
1. You can use the die and marker.
2. You can do this systematically:
   - Week 3: do the red questions.
   - Week 6: blue questions
   - Week 9: lavender questions
   - Week 12: green questions

1. The oldest person in the group asks the first question.
2. Everybody makes **comments** and asks **follow-up questions,** and asks **What about you?**
3. After EVERYBODY answers (about 5 - 10 minutes), roll the die and ask another question.
4. Each question is designed to start a conversation. If a conversation starts, **GO WITH IT!** Forget the game.
5. The first group to finish makes an F. If you finish quickly, you did not ask many follow-up questions.

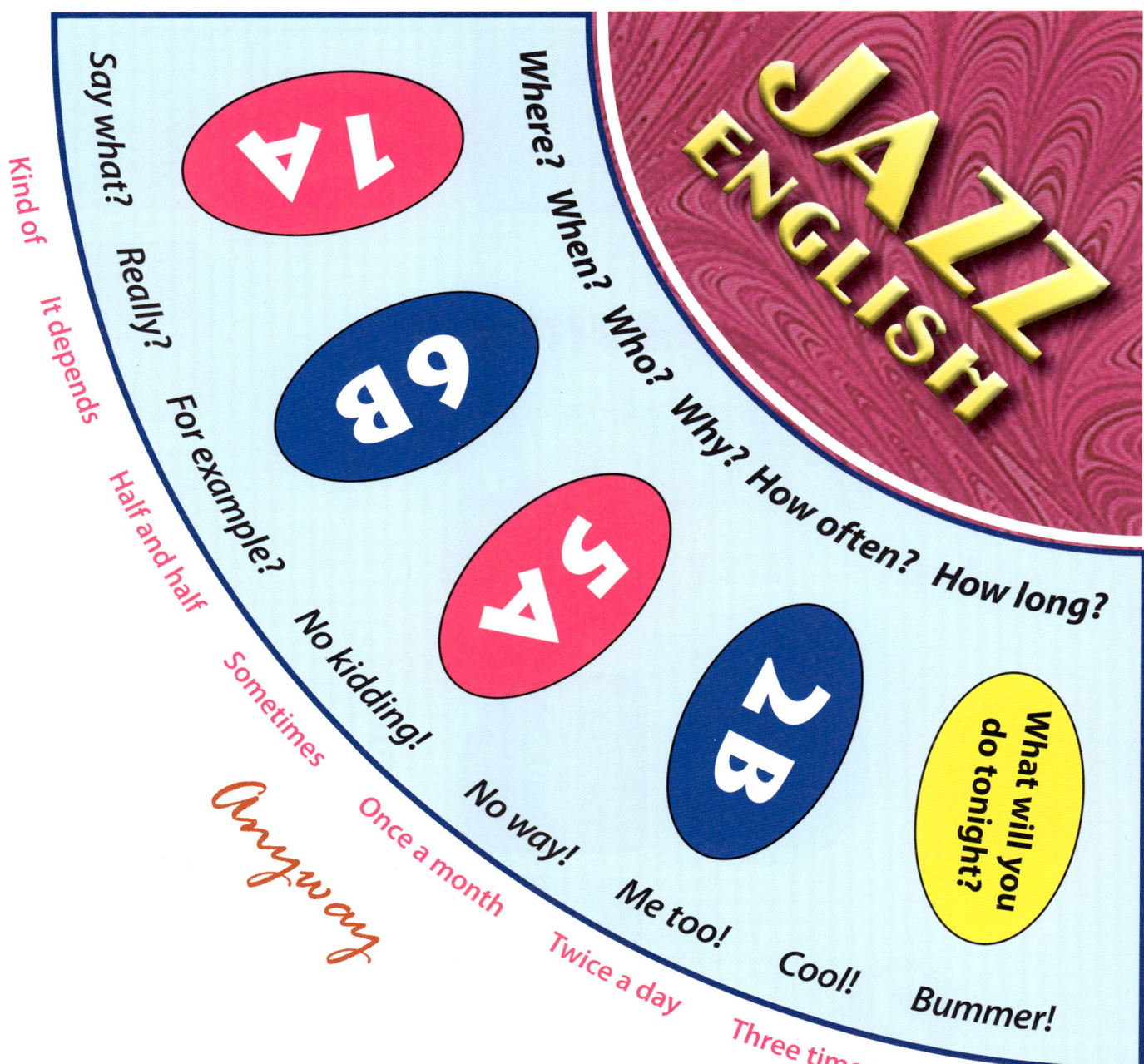

What about you?

DIRECTIONS

There are eight units in the book.

1. Each unit has A & B Conversation Starter questions.
   Page A and B each have 8 questions. *Got it?*

2. If you see 1A, that means ask a question from Unit 1, page A.
   If you see 5B, that means ask a question from Unit 5, page B. *Got it? OK!*

3   **The oldest person starts.**
    Open your book and ask a 3A question (any question from Unit 3, page A).
    Make comments and ask follow-up questions. Ask WHAT ABOUT YOU?
    After everybody answers the question, roll the die.
    If it lands with 3 up, move the marker up 3 times, and ask a 4B question.

4   **If a conversation starts, go with it.**

WHAT ABOUT YOU?

④ When? Where? Who? How? Why? How long? What time? How often?

- Your favorite TV show?
- Your favorite foreign movie star? Korean?
- Your favorite sport to play? To watch?
- Stay up all night studying? Drinking?
- Your favorite western restaurant Food?
- Travel abroad?
- Your favorite TV commercial? Which commercial do you hate?
- What you will do next vacation?
- What you did last vacation?
- Your favorite holiday?

③ Anyway

- Your schedule this semester?
- A country you would like to visit?
- How do you relax?
- Do you have a driver's license?

Again please. Louder please. Really? No kidding. Me too! Cool. Neat. Bummer. Say what? You're kidding! No way! Yeah, right! Get outta town! When pigs fly. In your dreams! And I'm Britney Spears.

- What you did last night?
- Your best vacation ever? Your worst?
- Miss school because you were sick?

⑤ If the question is in front of you, YOU read it

Whose turn?

- Where you live?
- Were you ever class president? Club president?

STOP

START

What you did last weekend?
What you will do tonight?
What you usually do after school?
Your plans for next weekend?
Your hobby?

③ Again please. Louder please.
Really? No kidding. Me too! Cool. Neat.
Bummer. Say what? You're kidding. No way!
Yeah, right! Get outta town! When pigs fly.
In your dreams! And I'm Britney Spears.

Where you were born?
Your favorite subject in high school?
Were you ever in a traffic accident?
Your favorite high school teacher?
Your favorite season?

④ **Make comments and Ask follow-up questions**

Anyway

How you get to school?

Fall asleep in class?
Your best birthday?
Do you believe in ghosts?

Finished already?
Dang, you talk fast.
Anyway.
Plan B. Start here, use another color and go the opposite way.

Spend more than 8 hours in a traffic jam?

Your high school?

③ Again please. Louder please.
Really? No kidding. Me too! Cool. Neat.
Bummer. Say what? You're kidding! No way!
Yeah, right! Get outta town! When pigs fly.
In your dreams! And I'm Britney Spears.

Do you like animals?

Travel on a big ship?

Fall asleep and miss your subway stop?

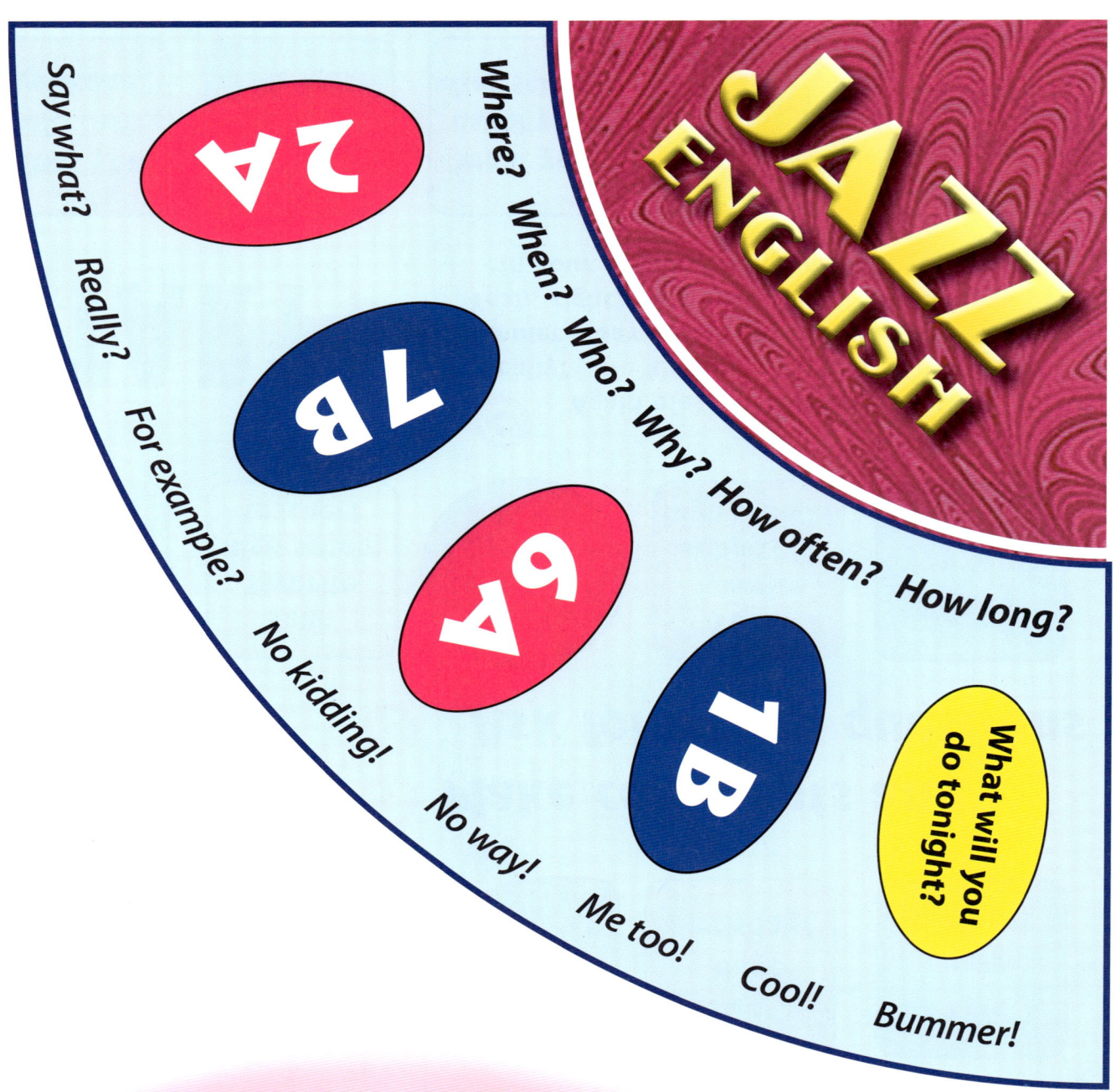

If your teacher was cool and bought you some chips, put most of them here.
(You can share a little.)

Anyway. What about you?

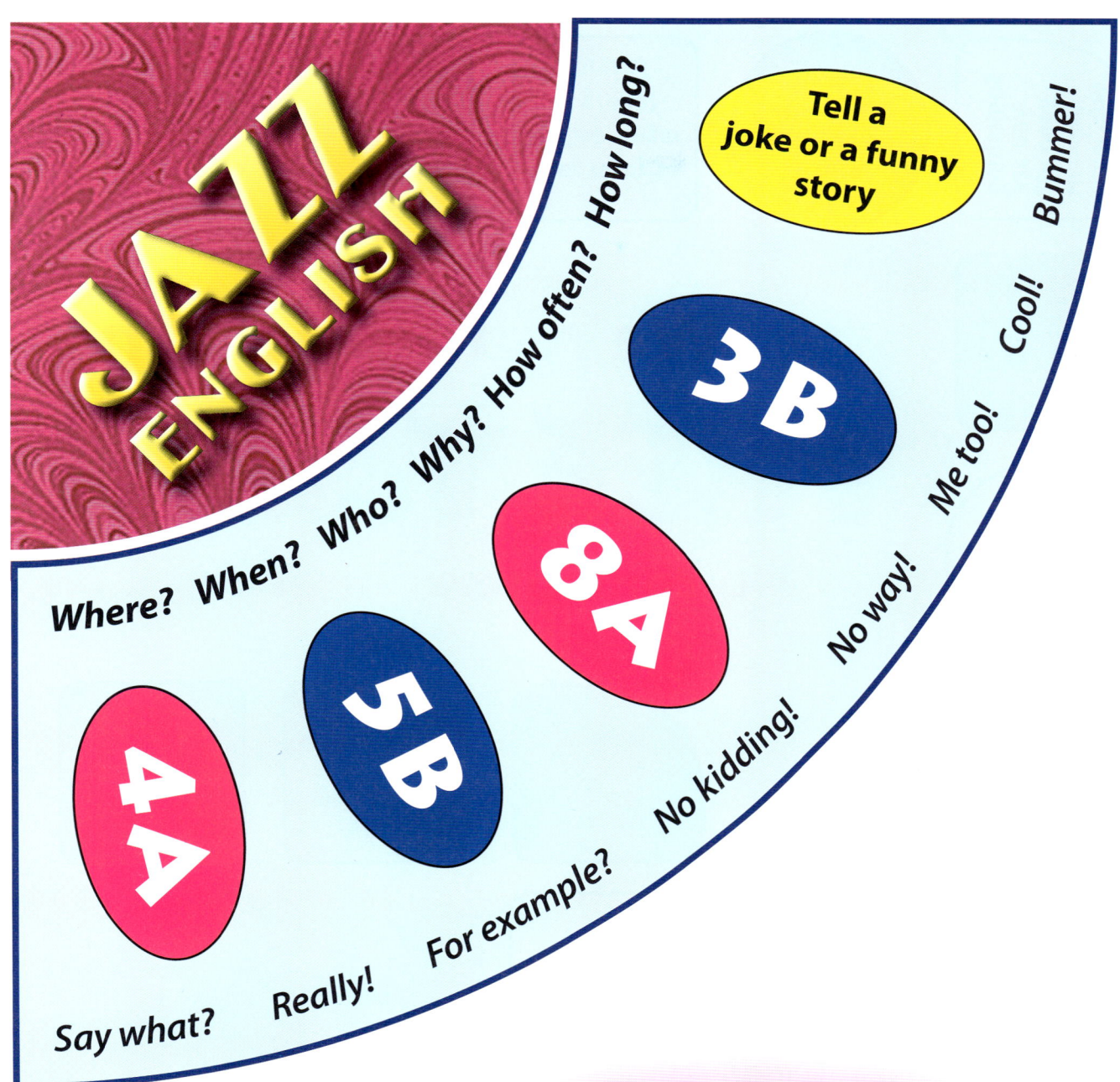

We're not goofing

FREE TALK!

No computers, Internet, CDs,

① If it's square, say

TELL US ABOUT

④ WHAT ABOUT YOU?

When? Where? Who? How? Why?
How long? What time? How often?

Board spaces (clockwise from top-left):

- Something you are good at? (music, art, math, sports)
- Win a contest or sporting event?
- Your favorite English singer or group? Korean?
- A job you want after graduating? (be realistic)
- Get badly cut or burned?
- Your favorite coffee shop or bar / pub
- What you drink, how much, & how often? Soju? Beer?
- Your pet, past or present?
- The biggest lie you ever told?
- Your website?
- Have a really scary dream?
- What you usually do on Saturday and Sunday?
- Get a really bad haircut?
- Your favorite kind of music? What kind of music do you hate?
- Your parents?
- Go on a strict diet?
- Something you worry about?

15 MAPS

1. WORLD	134
2. USA	136
3. KOREA	138
4. SEOUL	140

Have you ever traveled abroad?

Where, when, who, how long?
Highlight where you have been.

135

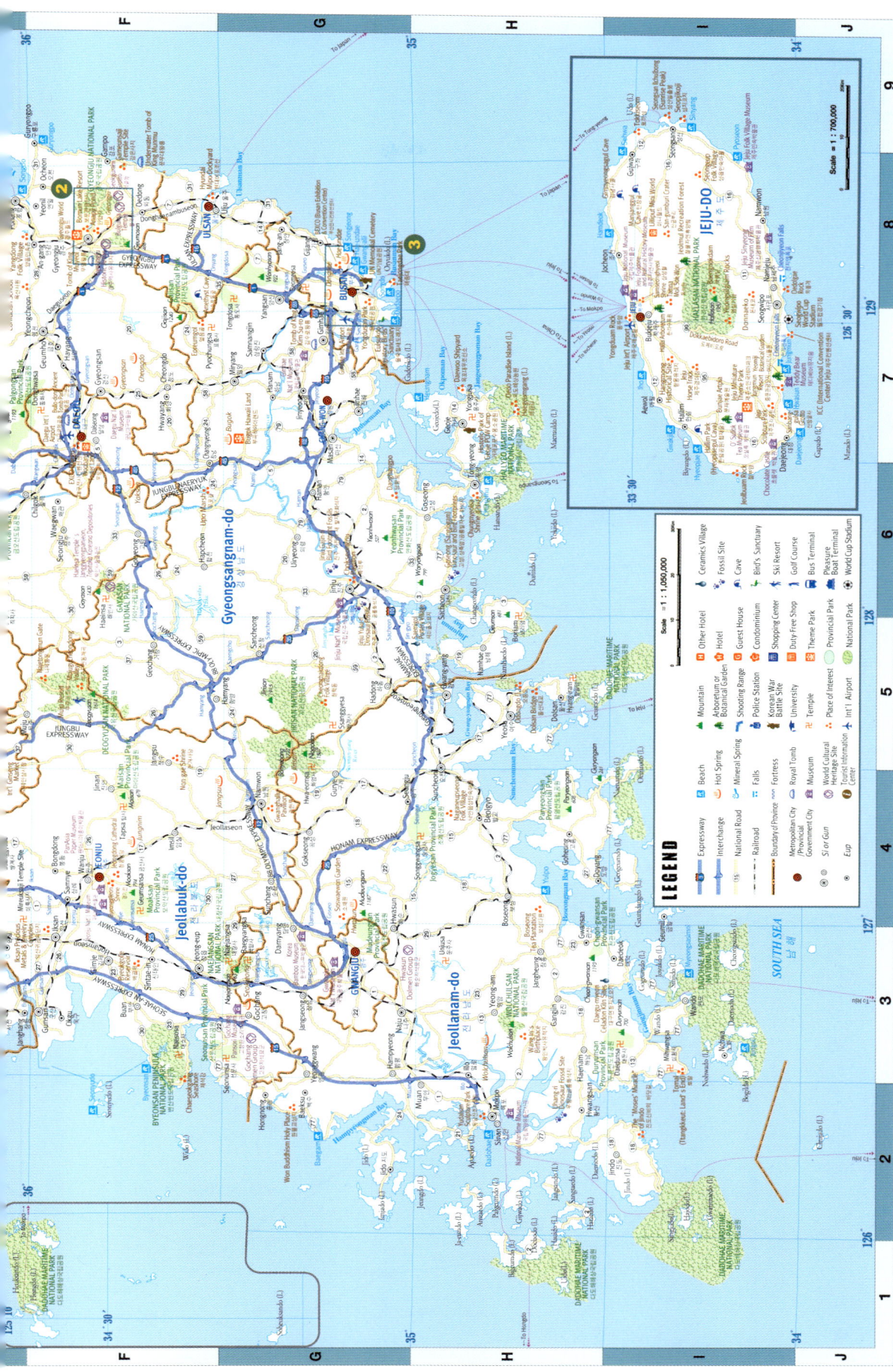